PSYCHODYNAMIC PSYCHOTHERAPY
WITH TRANSACTIONAL ANALYSIS

PSYCHODYNAMIC PSYCHOTHERAPY WITH TRANSACTIONAL ANALYSIS
Theory and Narration of a Living Experience

Anna Emanuela Tangolo

Translated by Adele Iozzelli and Kate Jones

KARNAC

First published in Italian in 2010 as *Psicoterapia psicodinamica con l'Analisi Transazionale: un'esperienza* by Felici Editore srl

A second edition was published in Italian in 2013

First published in English in 2015 by
Karnac Books Ltd
118 Finchley Road
London NW3 5HT

British Library Cataloguing in Publication Data

A C.I.P. for this book is available from the British Library

ISBN-13: 978-1-78220-155-7

Typeset by V Publishing Solutions Pvt Ltd., Chennai, India

Printed in Great Britain

www.karnacbooks.com

For ease of reading "she" is used throughout for the counsellor or therapist and "he" for the client or patient, but, at any point, the opposite gender can be substituted

CONTENTS

ACKNOWLEDGEMENTS

First and foremost, I would like to thank Franco Bertozzi, my husband and life companion, and supporter of all of my undertakings. I am in his debt for this book, above all for his frequent metaphors about the sea, sailing, and anchors, as well as for his passion for anthropology, and for imparting to me that intelligent and curious attitude of his towards those he encounters in his travels.

I also wish to thank Anna Massi, with whom I share a passion for the teaching of psychotherapy at the PerFormat school, for reading what I have written and for expressing her learned opinion of it.

I recall with fondness and esteem my colleagues of the Rome supervisory group, with whom I discuss the many topics dealt with in this book.

Thanks also go to Michele Novellino, my mentor for over twenty years, for having passed on to me his precious knowledge and his passion for psychotherapy and for Transactional Analysis (TA).

I remember with affection Carlo Moiso, the teacher who first spoke to me with passion about TA and whom we recently lost, but who has left a profound mark on so many of us.

In particular, I thank my patients, who teach me to listen, and to Terry, for her valuable reflections on group psychotherapy.

A special thanks to Adele Iozzelli and Kate Jones for the English translation of this book and to Silvia Rosa for her precious help in the editing process.

Last but not least, I want to thank Lorenzo, my secretary, for his daily support of my work and for the patience with which he faces each new task, together with our colleagues at PerFormat.

ABOUT THE AUTHOR

Anna Emanuela Tangolo is a psychotherapist and director of the PerFormat Psychotherapy Specializing School (Pisa and Catania, Italy). She is accredited by the European Association for Transactional Analysis (EATA) as a certified transactional analyst (CTA) and as a teaching and supervising transactional analyst (TSTA). In 2012 she founded PerFormat Salute, a professional network for the promotion of psychophysical health involving over eighty professionals—counsellors, psychologists, psychotherapists, psychiatrists—in over twenty polyfunctional centres all around Italy.

PREFACE

Michele Novellino

Most of us have, for many years, been waiting for Anna Emanuela Tangolo to write about her long and intense activity as a psychotherapist, counsellor, and trainer: it is therefore my great pleasure to be involved in this event with these few lines of my own.

Her book suggests a personalised approach to the world of the transactional analytical literature, which is somewhat flooded with works extremely close to being hypertechnical. The background to this work highlights what the experience of being a transactional analyst consists in: the idea of "being" intended as the "foundation" of "being able to do", which leads the reader back to the original principle of the founder of Transactional Analysis, Eric Berne.

The experience of "being a therapist" is related in this book with a style that illustrates and exemplifies what is intended to be conveyed: the therapist is involved in a narration, as Jim Allen would say, which is the patient's script. Emanuela "narrates" her own way of being a therapist and a trainer, and in doing this she adds her own style, her own culture, books, and films, showing the furniture of her office, and thus offering a model for her readers—for students, who can learn how important it is to determine their own style, and for experienced psychotherapists, who can think over some of their attitudes which may be stereotyped and crystallised.

The sense of "being" a therapist is considered of prime importance at every phase of therapy and counselling, from welcoming the client at the first meeting—which must be friendly without neglecting the rigour of the setting—to the contract: Berne's techniques are dealt with thoroughly in this book, while the narrative style chosen to characterise its plot is maintained.

The "patient" is described first of all as a "person" who suffers and asks for help, and the many cases described make the book somehow a novel, one of those novels described by Emanuela as an essential element for the growth of every psychotherapist.

Where the patient is first of all a person, he or she is consequently considered part of a social network, of this historical period, of a rapidly changing world. This element is underlined, examined, and illustrated with humanity and sensitiveness.

Here, the sense of "group" becomes clear, the context in which Transactional Analysis was born and must continue to flourish. The group is a re-enactment of archaic experiences, which leads back to Berne's concept of imago, and intertwining relationships where one can find oneself. The latter is a process vital to our patients, and nor must it be forgotten by the therapist, who may otherwise be/become too technical or neutral—which is desirable as long as it does not turn into a lack of sensitiveness.

In this research, Emanuela dedicates the right space to the analysis of dreams, seen as a powerful chance for the therapist–patient alliance to explore those levels of depth of self-knowledge which today are required, after two decades of "brief therapy" marketing which was supposed—in the opinion of many of those involved—to become generic psychotherapy.

This book represents a very effective and enjoyable tool, which intends not to replace, but to integrate with, a more technical literature, and it is really gratifying for me to satisfy Emanuela's request to write the introduction, given our long-term friendship.

INTRODUCTION

In my own words ...

I have been a psychologist for twenty-five years and a psychotherapist for almost twenty. Being a psychotherapist, and thus curing through words and Transactional Analysis, is my main activity. Even more than this, my job represents my being. I like dealing with counselling and training. These are fields of psychology where you often feel satisfied and successful as you take part in your students' and clients' achieving of their goals.

I love this job, and every time I stop to think, reflect, study, or write, a thousand faces and stories come to my mind; so many meetings with people who have been definitely relevant in my life. People come to see me as a psychotherapist and bring along their sufferings, uneasiness, some symptoms, a problem, a confused and sometimes conflictual situation or event, or a mourning they have to cope with. As a counsellor, I often meet people who are questioning the choices they've made in their lives, who are at a turning point, asking for support for a deeper understanding of themselves. Although cases are different, the beginning is always the same. I let the person in and I listen. The first step is very important. The place where the interview takes place is serene, quiet, peaceful, characterised by warm colours, surrounded by green and nature outside. The space of the office is defined as a living room which reveals the therapist's soul and mirrors my personality. However, there also has to be an empty space, so as to allow the other person in, a sober place where the person who arrives can stop for a while and enjoy a healthy break. Thus, when he arrives, someone will welcome and listen to him.

Listening is a deep process. It means meeting the other person, with his attitude, clothes, and smell, the way he looks at the world, sighs or keeps silent.

Then comes the tale, the narration: a brief story, a problematic event or the story of his life. At this moment, the patient himself is the narrator and the professional. I learn, smell, feel, try to have access to the world of meanings, emotions, feelings, in the film or the novel I'm being introduced to. There is a narrative structure which is gradually revealed. Actually, two stories often arrive together, one conveyed by the words, the other revealed by the body that is also communicating. Listening thus also becomes the meeting between two people, an interaction characterised by feedback and observations.

"So, you are telling me that …"

"I've seen that every time you refer to your stress, you touch and pinch your neck. Is there a connection between these two behaviours?"

Reading novels and analysing their structure, and watching films and plays, has taught me, at this phase, much much more than psychopathology.

I meet a person who talks about himself, and I love listening to stories, watching films, meeting people. I often notice that these narrations do not contain beauty or a sense of poetry, the depth of ethics and philosophy, which give me so much pleasure, meaning, and peace at the same time.

I believe that these stories are often narrated with poor expressiveness and a mediocre view that makes them seem boring, banal, or empty, even in their tragic or happy traits, which cannot be appreciated. Some people do not have a well-organised tale, rich in meaning. It is like watching a film without music, or rather the "making of" the scenes without a storyline, the plot that the final editing process gives the story.

Sometimes, when I get bored, I tell myself: maybe he gets bored too, maybe he walks all the time in the same garden and sees the same tree.

Very few people can observe the very same tree all their lives and make something pleasant and poetical of it. For some, psychotherapy is like making a movie or writing a novel from scattered information, and accompanying the story with good music which will give the protagonist a chance to become a passionate spectator or reader of the story that is being told. Directing and editing this film is a four-handed task; it will depend on the skills of both therapist and patient to build that harmony which we define as "healing". Some people come to therapy as if they were Italo Calvino's baron in the trees or cloven viscount, frightened by the world and relationships, and they ask me for educational support rather than therapy. These people need to find the strength to go back into the world, to face life. Usually, they have to face a lot of changes. Therapy appears to be some kind of training to be ready for what is unknown, unforeseen, new. Some people arrive with a wound to be healed: there has been a trauma, or some painful and sometimes sudden event that the mind has not managed to cope with or process, and the feelings are blocked, frozen in a moment which no longer exists. In this case, it is necessary to intervene both delicately and powerfully, as it is necessary to guide the person firmly towards processing, rather than negotiating, the event. The lost balance cannot be retrieved, one cannot go back, one can only move on and find a new balance. It is clear how this differs from a surgical orthopaedic intervention and the postural rehabilitation that one has to undertake after the bones have healed. In the psyche, something similar occurs, and the psychotherapist must be aware of the phase of the process at which her intervention occurs. Is there, then, a difference between psychotherapy and an educational path, between accompanying the patient along the direction he wants to follow and restructuring the map that leads there? When we stop together with the patient to draw the map to reach a certain place that we want to get to (i.e., when we accept his initial request), we may find out that that is impossible reach (e.g., "I don't want to suffer for love ever again"). In this case, the patient has to be able to choose to change his destination and direction ("I want to face, in a healthy way, the suffering that I may encounter"). This, however, is achieved along the way.

In TA we define this way as the difference between the patient's request and the contract: the contract between therapist and patient consists in defining together a reachable objective, and often the process undertaken in order to define the contract already represents, in itself, a resolution. This because establishing a reachable realistic objective means that he has already recovered from most of his current neuroses.

While I listen to the patient's request in order to make a good contract with him, I ask myself: what does this person really need? And what can *I* do for him? Does his story have to do with anything that psychopathology has taught me? In this person's suffering can I find some rigidity which can be explained in scientific language? Can that particular symptom be associated with a system that has already been observed? And, has his derangement been previously observed and studied in other people? Or, can his difficulty in living and establishing relationships with the world around him be rooted in the story of his first relevant relationships? Is there, in this person's disorganisation, an explanation that enables me to reach a turning point and lead him to a more satisfactory balance? Psychotherapy follows this pattern. Then comes the diagnostic process and the definition of the treatment plan. For me it is helpful to structure the setting this way: can this person benefit from group therapy, or does he need to be listened to in individual meetings? And I will be there, with him, for a time previously agreed upon. I am like a parent who looks after the other, who takes care of him at a particular moment of his life. I usually get to know patients' parents through what they tell me or project on to me. I listen to myself, and I see that some affectionate gesture is not perceived, sincere interest is disregarded, an appreciation becomes a criticism. Thus starts my dialogue with the parents of the patients who come to me and with those scared, inhibited, or wild children that these parents dealt with. The adult before me does not realise to what extent he is actually representing so much of his story, albeit in the microcosm and in the short time of the interview. I do listen, however; I listen to what *I* say as well, and in a few words I ask, I give observations and impressions as feedback, thus beginning, together with the patient, to choose a new thread and to weave a different pattern. Then, sometimes, time passes, sessions are repetitive, and to me they seem all alike, without any changes. I get discouraged—maybe I cannot help this person, or maybe I am too impatient. I often think of Penelope, who undoes at night what she then weaves again during the day, so that she will never finish her work and time remains suspended in the hope that the man for whom she has been waiting, for so many years, will come back. Sometimes, this may happen too. Then, entering a group helps me break the spell of interminable therapy, of the fear of change that some patients suddenly feel, and due to which we would both be trapped in the web, like Arachne after she challenged the goddess. Thus, the groups: I particularly like working with groups; I consider groups as a privileged laboratory for change and a pathway to healing.

The group is a mother's uterus, warmer and larger than mine, a warm and friendly cave where I am priestess and fire. I know that and I like it. In the group there is, however, the central nucleus of plurality too: there is the symbol of the father who makes the rules and defines the possibility to live together peacefully around the fire. There is the possibility to share food with the brothers and there are brothers to play with, to spend time with, explore together, and sleep embracing each other. In the group, one goes back to an archaic, primordial state in which desires and fears re-emerge. And even before that, desires and fears, non-differentiation, the fusion from which we all then later take our own shape as individuals. In the group, those who put themselves in the hands of others, running the risk of such an important action, find a great opportunity: of course, the great interpersonal experiences re-emerge, and so do the thoughts and feelings that characterise us; the dramas and the dreams of belonging and of becoming part of something are re-lived—competition, definition of self through the others' looks and dialogue. In the group, one first of all looks for one's own place, then for a mirror in which to look at oneself, then, finally, for the way to face one's life. In the group, one looks for shelter and support, which will then be interiorised and will enable that person to separate and leave. I feel joyful when I see people come back to life with enthusiasm and energy, become fecund and constructive, love and hope again. How can all this be explained, since it is my life more than my job? This book has been written because of the need to tell doctors and psychologists who study psychotherapy about my passion for this job and about the basic structure and process of Transactional Analysis psychotherapy. One hundred years after Berne's birth and forty years after his death, his teachings are still deeply valid and helpful for those who choose to work as psychotherapists. The number of schools is increasing, his books are republished and clinical research on the issue of transactional-analytical metapsychology has just begun. Concepts such as ego states, transactions, games, and script are deeply rich, both in meaning to be explored and in possibilities for practical applications.

As innovative contributions to the technique of psychotherapy, the clinical tools of Berne's therapy group, and techniques of intervention such as therapeutic operations with great focus on the interview—seen as a linguistic interweaving of an experience to send stimuli to the patient in order to re-structure his intrapsychic world through rigorous and precise inputs, analysable in sequences—are still there to be studied and shared with the scientific and professional community.

CHAPTER ONE

Being a counsellor and a psychotherapist*

It is a major task of trainers, psychotherapists, business consultants, or occupational psychologists to develop deep, significant practice in order to make human relationships better, the world a friendlier place, and social relationships healthier and more ecological.

My considerations are a reflection on our vision of mankind, and therefore on the value system we teach in Transactional Analysis (TA), and on those aspects of the model of intervention that, we may say, involve different elements of what we experience every day as psychotherapists and counsellors.

While elaborating and reflecting on this text, I was perfectly aware that I would be talking to people specialised in training and professionally concerned with health. There are clinical psychologists among us—psychotherapists, counsellors—and also business psychologists, who use Transactional Analysis as an instrument to improve the well-being of organisations.

---

*Pisa, First PerFormat Conference, 11 October 2008.

Transactional Analysis was developed in the late 1950s by Eric Berne, an American psychiatrist and psychoanalyst who died in 1970 and whose 100th birthday was celebrated in 2010.

What can Berne still teach us through Transactional Analysis?

I searched through my memories so I could tell you what it was about Transactional Analysis that attracted me and what made me choose this model among so many others. When we have to choose a field of specialisation, our choice is often determined by the influence of meaningful encounters, books that have particularly impressed us, or personal experiences, like a psychotherapeutic path that enables us to get directly acquainted with a model and a philosophy of health.

Similarly, my encounter with Transactional Analysis reminds me of significant moments of my youth, and these memories are closely intertwined with stories, experiences, important people, and readings that affected me deeply.

After studying philosophy and psychology at university, I became acquainted with Transactional Analysis thanks to the teachings of a psychotherapist who trained me to work in therapeutic communities in which, in the early eighties, young people who were drug addicted or affected by life-sickness—so widespread among adolescents—were treated. This is how I learned about the teachings of Eric Berne, who was the first to experiment with group therapy.

Eric Berne, whom we know as the founder of our school, was basically a friendly psychiatrist and an anthropologist.

Berne says that "To say Hello rightly is to see the other person, to be aware of him as a phenomenon, to happen to him and to be ready for him to happen to you" (Berne, 1972, pp. 3–4). He then compares the kind of greeting smile that one should have with the one that children and adults on the Fiji Islands have.

In *What Do You Say After You Say Hello?* Berne writes: "The people who show this ability to the highest degree are the Fiji Islanders, for one of the rare jewels of the world is the genuine Fijian smile. It starts slowly appears, it illuminates the whole face, it rests there long enough to be clearly recognised" (Berne, 1972, p. 4).

Later he will write, in this same introduction, that often we therapists and clinical psychologists do take care of all that is not this spontaneous smile, and of all that prevents people from noticing and perceiving this spontaneous smile. We therapists take care of those who can no longer smile at others and cannot trust a spontaneous smile, those who no longer enjoy a child's spontaneity and frankness.

As for the value system I mentioned earlier, in my reflection on values I have searched for support from the field of philosophy—as in my personal history I discovered Berne and psychology after studying philosophy, and in my student days, twenty years ago, I was accompanied by a woman who was very important for my education: Hannah Arendt.

In a book I deeply love, *The Human Condition*, Hannah Arendt says something that I find extremely helpful for us: men, and not Man, inhabit the earth and the world, and thus she says that the human condition is plural.

Plurality is the law of the earth. When she says plurality, therefore, she actually means that the importance we give to the group and relationships is not at all a secondary dimension of our being human. On the contrary, this dimension is primary and specific to ourselves as human beings.

So, if we compare Arendt's philosophy with Berne's ideas, we find a deep correspondence in their thoughts about mankind.

Berne had this great, powerful intuition: he did not consider the intrapsychic as a dimension of an individual separated from the rest of the world. On the contrary, he considered the relational dimension as the constitutive dimension of human beings.

When Berne spoke about transactions, when he told us about Parent, Adult, Child, when he spoke about groups, when he described human personality as something which is built in a dimension of relational attachment, he talked about something that Arendt describes as specific to the human condition.

There is another concept Hannah Arendt expressed in *The Human Condition* that I also found inspiring for us: the *activa* dimension of human living is, in several aspects, more important than what, in the past, was defined as the contemplative or meditative dimension.

When Arendt speaks about *"vita activa"*, she is saying something very important: she distinguishes labour, work, and action, and she defines labour as the lowest form of *"vita activa"*. People labour in order to survive, out of need, to get food. Labour is therefore necessary, but it is the minimal form of action that enables people to be part of the world.

She says that working actually means transforming the things of the world so as to make the world friendlier. Our products, our factories, our transformations accordingly represent the carrying out of such a transformation of the world.

She also says, however, that men truly become human beings through the dimension of acting. Why do we act? We act because we are human beings.

What is meant, though, by acting?

Acting means taking an initiative, beginning, *archein* in Greek; beginning means leading, initiating something.

Acting, we might say, means creating and co-creating freely, building and creating the city of humans, and it also means expressing oneself freely and generating art, spirituality, culture, exchange, games.

It means, after all, that expressing ourselves through relational dialogue and action is inevitable and necessary for us humans—just as relationships are fundamental for us. Labouring is not specific to our being, or fundamental: it is just part of survival: while acting—meant as expressing oneself, creating, inventing, playing in the sense of *ludus*, the creative game, art, the creation of spiritual worlds and culture—really is essential for us.

Going back to what I consider fundamental values, both in Transactional Analysis and in the history we want to have as transactional analysts, I hope we are not mere workers—according to Arendt's definition of working, that is, making the world a friendlier place—although this would, in itself, be quite a significant action. I wish we could aim at being people of action, in the noblest meaning of the term: people involved in politics, culture, who help others express freely their artistic and spiritual dimension—which Maslow (1962) considered to be of the highest values—and who therefore accompany others along a path towards a development which implies growth and development for ourselves too.

Speaking, communicating, and acting, in the sense of creating, are thus the constitutive dimensions of a plural person, because when people are free, they talk, play, create, love.

We are relational beings, therefore: we know that we were born from a relationship, a love relationship. We know that a hug brings us to life, and that dialogue enables us to grow into the world. Berne used to say: "We have a biological hunger for structure, food and strokes."

We are aware that food, too, is received in an attachment relationship: we need to be recognised and accepted by a human group, but we also know—and here Berne was great—that we need structure and we need to know how to significantly pass our time. This is *agere*, acting, Arendt's "*vita activa*", something very different from hiding our real selves all the time, losing the sense and the meaning of things. On the contrary, it consists in searching for real sense and meaning.

In his description of the concept of time structuring, Berne quotes activity and intimacy as the most important elements and aims of social time structuring.

I have tried to establish a connection between Berne's concept of activity and Hannah Arendt's concept of acting. Actually, I don't know whether Berne knew Arendt, or at least I have no evidence from the quotes in his biography, but I have found that what she writes in *The Human Condition* is extraordinarily and singularly close to his thoughts.

The Human Condition is a book that was appreciated belatedly, a book from the end of the 1950s, the time when Berne was beginning to write and to define Transactional Analysis as a separate dimension, a daughter of psychoanalysis but developed autonomously. I find that Berne's concept of activity is extraordinarily close to what Arendt calls "*vita activa*".

As a matter of fact, TA is not merely a technique of intervention but also a philosophy about mankind, especially in some of its main assumptions, in which we identify with Berne, for example, when he says that every human being has a right to his or her place in the world and is naturally oriented to life and well-being. This is his idea of nature, of physis: that people are naturally oriented to life and well-being.

Every human being is characterised by "projectuality": everyone needs to define himself in terms of identity, to have a safe place in the world and also to challenge his certainties in order to build his future and leave his own mark on the world. I have always associated Berne with Heidegger's existentialism and Karl Jaspers' thinking. Heidegger and Jaspers deeply influenced Hannah Arendt: Arendt communicated with Heidegger and Jaspers all her life.

It is the active life, acting, and thus the free and creative part of man, which characterises human beings: in TA we talk about autonomy, in contrast with the concept of script, meant as limit and restriction.

Identity and those certainties that make life predictable may become a prison due to a life script which restrains us and does not accept novelties; a cage, an identity, a limit, repetition compulsion, and, at the same time, the safe sensation of "I am the person who …" and "Life is what I already know and can foresee".

The need for autonomy, the search for freedom, the urge to plan and explore, however, invite us human beings to go beyond the boundaries of what has already been experienced. In everyone's life the burden and the consistency of the past can be felt: "I am the son or daughter of this person … I was born in this historical moment, I am the son or daughter of this time of crisis, transformations, and change, but not even all this can entirely describe me."

And yet, to quote Gibran, in our soul there is also a future direction we don't yet know.

We are born from intimacy, from a hug, we experience symbiosis, the attachment relationship, we separate in order to be defined as individuals, then as adults we find in the couple a new kind of intimacy, and the couple is the couple of love, of cultural and spiritual intimacy, of deep dialogue.

This same intimacy can sometimes be experienced in counselling and therapy, in a relationship that redefines us as relational beings and enables us to rediscover the love for ourselves when this has been lost. Another important dimension, though, is the dimension of journey.

As a matter of fact, the important intimacy of the dual relationship is not enough, as the dimension of journey is very significant in our lives: we need to be on a journey during our growth, we need to go from what is predictable to what is unknown and try to face explorations that send us towards new lands and experiences. Maybe you know these words, spoken by Gibran's Prophet:

> Your children are not your children.
> They are the sons and daughters of Life's longing for itself.
> They come through you
> But not from you.
> And though they are with you, yet they belong not to you.
> You may give them your love
> But not your thoughts
> For they have their own thoughts.
> You may house their bodies
> But not their souls

For their souls dwell in the house of tomorrow,
Which you cannot visit, not even in your dreams.
(Gibran, 1991, p. 22)

I have chosen this poem, which I think we all know, to describe how growing up means going towards new worlds.

In our job, respecting what is unknown, unpredictable, what the soul of the people we encounter is yet to be, implies being for them both a discreet guide and a close and careful listener, so that those we meet will not model themselves on us but will instead discover themselves, discover a path that will lead them to an unknown place.

If we are good counsellors or therapists, those who come out of our studies and training courses will not resemble us: they will take on their own colours, clothes, thoughts, which may even be more positive, genial, and important than what we were able to offer them.

Our wish as trainers is to be good incubators, a good place, a seedbed where the seeds, in a particular atmosphere, have a chance to germinate. That is what our training rooms and familiar environments are, because environments where people are treated must be places where the sprouts can germinate and—once they are ready—enter the soil to produce something much greater and more complex than the little seed we hosted.

People who turn to us as counsellors often feel imprisoned, and look for freedom and peace of mind. People turn to us because they feel some kind of uneasiness, and their request is to achieve peace and quiet: the calm we help them to achieve, however, has nothing to do with a drowsy condition, typical of passivity. This kind of interior calm also contains the unrest of growth. We want to accompany people along a path that will lead them to be able to cope with the healthy unrest due to their growing up, their being real people.

Being alive and spiritual creatures, human beings cannot live in complete rest. In their lives, they need to dedicate space and time equally to a condition of both rest and unrest.

Another very influential personality of our time, Daniel Stern, would say that the purpose of counselling and psychotherapy is to enable a person to experience new balances: people often attend counselling or psychotherapy to obtain some kind of change, and the main assumption is that such change, as Stern wrote in 2004 "is based on lived experience. In and of itself, verbally understanding, explaining or narrating something is not sufficient to bring about change. There must also be an actual experience, a subjectively lived happening. An event must be *lived*, with feelings and actions taking place in real time, in the real world, with real people, in a moment of presentness" (Stern, 2004, p. xiii).

Over the last few years, I have learned to appreciate and use the Greek phrase *kairos*, which means "the present moment, the favourable moment" as, while reading Stern for the second time, I found in this concept a great enlightening intuition; the place of conversation, the place of therapy, and of some important moments in our training, are, as a matter of fact, *kairos* moments, moments that in the here and now enable us to guess that life can be different, that we can reach intimacy, discover our intelligence and the vital energy that we think has died down, and find out that we can really follow a fortunate path that will lead us to a change.

Thus, the group is the privileged tool and the most suitable place for training. Training in TA is developed in the group; in psychotherapy and counselling this is the privileged tool. Becoming part of a group is indeed a fundamental choice of intervention for us, and these are therefore our values, the choice of intervention, the group. Why do we consider the group the most helpful tool of intervention? Because entering a group often implies modifying the primary scene a person has in his own head—what Berne called "imago"—acquiring new stimuli, actors, themes.

We know that the group comes as something of a shock, a place where one has to face the world, the school, the games of childhood and adolescence, the sexual dynamics of one's growth, the operative, creative, and intellectual challenges of life.

These very challenges are what we hope people will not run away from, so that they can get over the traumas of their primary group experiences, when such traumas brought about lack of self-assurance and negative self-esteem.

The group can be a constructive experience in several contexts, especially during training periods. In TA we teach how to handle classes and training groups because this provides tools to create environments where the atmosphere is pleasant and therefore favourable to learning. The teacher or the facilitator trained in TA checks on both *what* is being done and *how* it is being done, since making people active during the learning process is strongly connected with the emotions aroused and the curiosity stimulated.

Counselling takes place in a group because dialogue within a group where people listen, share, and also learn from each other, is a powerful counselling tool.

In firms and associations, the meetings based on counselling methods become an effective tool for reflection and generative negotiation. Meetings are one of the most critical moments in work-places: people want to get meetings over with as soon as possible, and meetings themselves often prove to be ineffective and even create deep uneasiness.

One of our activities in business consultancy consists in turning the meetings into group works where ideas are actually generated, effectiveness, punctuality, and respect for people are achieved, and where people can finally feel that sense of personal satisfaction which is Arendt's "acting".

Berne developed TA as group therapy, a particular kind of group in which the script can be acted in its primary protocol and one can become aware of the script apparatus. This particular group creates the conditions for a corrective and re-decisional experience ultimately different from the attachment models. It particularly allows one to reinforce and energise the experience of the here and now (*kairos*), to acquire stimuli thanks to both resonance with others and awareness, and to experience new solutions to old problems through learning from the here-and-now dimension of the relationships and of the group field.

The group thus provides a context in which to repair and correct, to learn to have relationships. If we are in a group, we learn to experience emotive resonance, to acquire empathy and sympathy for the others, to co-ordinate with the others: I'm thinking of Aldo, who walked into doors and couldn't dance, or Elisa, who spoke while others were speaking, without even looking at them.

These are the changes we can observe and appreciate in a group experience: we see that these people no longer stumble when they walk, manage to co-ordinate themselves with others while they speak and look other people in the eye. We see how this represents a radical turn in their relational attitude and, therefore, maybe even in their chances of being happy and serene in their lives.

We also experience that whenever we have a tendency for fusion or symbiosis, it is necessary to limit our emotive resonance. We experience that we can still feel surprised and that even in our adulthood we are still capable of learning.

Since a transactional analyst knows and uses group methods, she is an expert who doesn't work isolated in her counselling or therapy study, but is constantly communicating and in touch with the scientific and professional community through contacts with international associations, constant updating, and exchange with others.

As Berne's disciples, we are anthropologists and therefore people who are curiously interested in encountering other human beings. We are part of a scientific community that questions its assumptions, seeks and needs confrontation; we are people who accept ethical and professional confrontation with our colleagues but who are also able to create inner spaces of silence and thought for ourselves.

A person who is able to be part of a group and to be with others must also be able to be alone, to reflect on her acting, let silence nurture her so to be able to keep listening to others.

In this perspective, Karl Jaspers (1969), psychiatrist, doctor, and philosopher, states that in existential communication being silent is a modus of communication. According to him, there is a moment to be silent within the continuity of a communicative process. In the pause thus inevitably created, one is inclined to waiting, and waits for the time for a reciprocal opening. Refraining in reciprocal certainty, choosing our look and our hands over the spoken word, is what is left in the moments of perfection of existential communication. Here, silence is the authentic word.

A counsellor, trainer, and therapist, as we all are, needs meditation, the space and silence of the desert and also pure and free game, smiles, music, dance, and colours.

At the end of her book on active political life, Arendt quotes Cato, an ancient Latin master who used to say: "Never is a man more active than when he does nothing, never is he less alone than when he is by himself" (Arendt, 1957, p. 325).

In this sense, the conciliation of these opposite concepts lies in a process of learning that needs to be experienced, on a path that is a professional and cultural path, made up of relationships, and is, therefore, also a spiritual path.

CHAPTER TWO

Psychotherapy with TA

The journey

Doing psychotherapy means starting a journey inside oneself, and along this path a good guide is necessary, as in a speleological exploration: one is entering the unknown areas of one's self and of interaction with others.

The time of psychotherapy interrupts the ordinary course of life and turns it into a moment of pause, reflection, research. Within the framework of the frantic rhythm of postmodern life, the time of therapy often represents the only pause in our hurried living, where little space is reserved for thinking and feeling.

For many of us, psychotherapy becomes a school where we can learn about the space and silence of the desert, about slowing down the frantic pace of our lives, like scuba-diving in the sea or hiking in the mountains. This experience often has an educative function: we rediscover how to breathe correctly, to listen and to be listened to, to get in touch with our own emotions and let them act as a compass to orient our behaviour.

Weekly interviews with the therapist naturally become like a mirror where we can see our own self, as well as a chance to experience deeper introspection and enhance our reflections on our self and on life.

The guide

The psychotherapist's role in the meetings is to provide a scheme of interpretation and analysis of data through helpful questions and close listening which foster, in the patient, reflections about himself and the will to exchange views about these with others. Besides, through the setting, and a dialogue that is intensely meaningful and at the same time respectful of personal spaces, is neutral, non-judgemental, the therapist enables the patient to experience a unique formative and curative experience.

According to such a view, the therapist is both a scientist and an anthropologist, a doctor and a shaman. Like a shaman from ancient times, the therapist smells and hears, is present in the meeting with all of the patient's senses. Through intuition, the therapist searches for the key issue of the uneasiness that restrains and blocks life, so as to open the door to a fresh breath of air, to change. Like a modern anthropologist, the therapist observes. Like a scientist, she analyses data and symptoms in the history of the patient. Like a doctor for the mind, the therapist leads the patient to restructure and reorder emotions and interpretations of human experience.

Conferring meaning on a history of difficulty, uneasiness, and suffering, being able to read the symptom and what the person communicates to those before him through this symptom, also means finding a path amidst brambles and finding logic and order in the confused material that characterises narrations, dreams, and diseases.

Acting on different levels, the therapist can cure: she listens—and this represents in itself a cure for a person who lives in solitude—and picks up and organises the broken pieces of the other's self, giving the other a chance to heal.

Besides, the therapeutic relationship becomes the place, space, and structure that protect from fear and sense of disintegration, and thus provides a modeling experience, like a new parenting and a new possibility of attachment.

This new attachment relationship, for those who are willing and in need, is a chance to rewrite their life scripts, re-deciding in a healthier way how to face life and, above all, how to choose strategies more effective than the archaic ones chosen during childhood.

The therapist is a person who can listen and who looks at the other through a child's curious and interested look, the deep and friendly look of a parent who welcomes him to the world, and the competent look of an adult who knows how the human soul and psyche work.

Siegel writes that:

> As self-states emerge over time, the mind has the challenge of integrating these relatively autonomous processes into a coherent whole. Psychotherapy can catalyze the development of such a core integrative process by facilitating dyadic states of resonance: right hemisphere to right hemisphere, left hemisphere to left hemisphere. In such a process, the mind of the patient (and that of the therapist) can become immersed in primary emotional states, while simultaneously focusing on reflective narrative explorations. Such affect attunement and reflective dialogue catalyze an internal, bilateral form of resonance within each member of the dyad. [...] This form of resonance may be at the core of an integrating process that permits emotion regulation across time and across self-states. It is from this state of cooperative activation that coherent narratives emerge, and through this process that the mind is able to achieve maximal complexity and thus stable self-organization. Psychotherapy is a complex process. [...] Our minds are complex systems. [...] It is a challenge, and a profound privilege, to keep an objective focus on a patient's emotional needs while at the same time allowing oneself as the therapist to join with the patient's evolving states of mind. (Siegel, 1999, pp. 334–335)

Different scripts, different ways to start therapy, different outcomes

When someone enters a psychotherapist's office for the first time, the therapist knows that that person might either have a constructive script, and be thus more inclined to be "cured" from his suffering, or be a person with a banal or destructive script, aiming at an unsatisfactory or even tragic life. The therapist knows how these scripts depend on the beliefs a person has created for himself according to his primary experiences of attachment and relationships.

Some beliefs enable us to step serenely into a friendly world where we feel we belong and where living is a natural, enjoyable passion, while some beliefs dramatically lead to a fight that is lost even before it has started, to resentment towards others and life itself.

These different beliefs originate within primary experiences of love or abandonment, agreement or conflict about space and existence.

Berne wrote that "the destiny of every human being is determined by what goes on inside his skull when he is confronted with what goes on outside his skull" and that "every person designs his own life" (Berne, 1972, p. 31).

In therapy it is easy to recognise how the script acts to affect and limit the adult's freedom.

Ciro's case

Ciro is a young man aged twenty-seven who comes for only one meeting, declaring he suffers from several disorders that make his life hard: he has difficulties in eating in public and is sometimes afraid of suffocating while he swallows, and, because of that, he excludes several foods from his diet. He is also afraid of leaving the gas stove on when he goes out and he tells me he sometimes wastes a lot of time checking that everything has been turned off.

He is single, works for a government administration outside his region, and commutes every week so that he can come back to his mother's every Friday. His mother is a very difficult person, described as an old woman who has always suffered from depression and severe persecution complexes, who heavily affected her two children's lives.

Ciro has an older sister, who is married and lives near them. Their father died of liver cirrhosis, he was an alcoholic. Ciro is an intelligent, sad man; he doesn't know what joy is. He regrets that he hasn't been able to realise his dream of becoming a magistrate because he had to leave university.

After this first meeting, I see him again ten years later, when he decides to undertake psychotherapy.

When he comes back, he tells me that many important things have happened: he fell in love with a psychologist and went to live with her; his mother committed suicide the previous year, blaming her two children for her anguish; and his sister has just died of a sudden brain cancer. Ciro is the only survivor. He tells me that when his mother died,

his obsessive-compulsive disorder (OCD) symptoms di:
that in that period he was depressed and decided to start t
had put off for years.

In this meeting, he gives me a photocopy of the note hi:
when she killed herself and tells me he wants me to keep it, ⌐υ ɯat one
day, if he feels better, together with me, he can burn it.

I accept his request, and we begin. Ciro will attend one year of individual therapy and four of group therapy. Over the years, he will make
the decision to sell the house of the suicide and find a new home, get
married and have a child, and take important decisions in his job. Most
importantly, he will buy himself a motorbike, start taking photos, and
organise dinners, parties, and real holidays. Ciro will burn his mother's
message during a session of group therapy.

For Ciro, it was very difficult to rest, sleep well, and relax, eat with
pleasure, laugh with his friends and enjoy their company. The dimension of pleasure in him was completely blocked, he did not feel he had
the right to feel well, his being alive was already enough!

Ciro slowly became aware of how violent and imprisoning an atmosphere he had been subdued to during his childhood; he had been a
mistreated child, had suffered deeply due to his mother's madness, but
had nonetheless found it very hard to separate from her.

When everybody in his family died, it was as if he expected he
would die too and follow them; however, the decision to come to group
therapy week after week and confer the dignity of a real dimension on
his life, opened for him the possibility to write a new script for himself.
During the last period he spent in the group, he used to say: "Now,
when I introduce myself, I talk about my son, my achievements, my
current life; before, I introduced myself by talking about funerals."

What happened during the course of therapy which made Ciro a
serene man? To what extent is his current balance due to our work or to
other events, such as love and his self-healing capacity?

We might say that Ciro was the only one destined to be saved from
his family nucleus; perhaps the fact that if he had separated from his
original nucleus he would have made it, after overcoming obstacles,
was already written in his script.

It is very difficult to answer these questions, and the reflections above
are quite likely valid.

The contribution of psychotherapy to Ciro's "healing" mainly con-
sisted in accompanying him in the restructuring of his internal Parent

(the system of rules and protection), which was rigid, crazy, and tended to manifest itself with persecutory attitudes towards others (he often quarreled with others and made himself strongly unpleasant) and himself (he didn't take care of himself, he wasn't considerate towards himself, had no self-respect, and did not allow himself to rest and have fun).

As Ciro discovered that his rules were too strict, he began to learn from the therapist, and from the group, "softer" and more permissive attitudes towards himself and others. He then began, like a child, to explore, behaviours he had never had (he was funny, he made jokes, he stopped to chat with others before and after the group, he even went out to eat with others before the therapy session).

All this contributed to restructuring his internal Parent, and, as he learned to give himself more permissions, the internal Child seemed to come back to the surface and to actively learn how to live.

In his Adult ego state, Ciro decided that he had the right to live and that what had happened wasn't his fault, and he gave himself permission to accept life's compensation when he had the courage, as he says, to have a son. Having a son would have been impossible at the beginning of therapy: Ciro claimed that his own blood was sick with depression, madness, probably tumours, and that it was necessary for his family to disappear. In his path towards change, Ciro has been accompanied by a very important relationship with the woman he then married and with whom he had his beloved son. Besides psychotherapy, there is thus a contribution from love in his path of reconstruction. However, the unanswered question is: would he have been able to keep trust and be open to love and intimacy with the passing of time if he had not deeply modified his script patterns and therefore his neuronal networks?

The mental process that led him to make these changes is what in TA is called decontamination and deconfusion. As he restructured his convictions, emotions were modified, and new experiences worked as a positive reinforcement to the relearning.

All this happened within a therapeutic relationship, in which Ciro emotively chose me as a substitute and reparative parent, and in which he chose the group as a new family-school where he could rediscover himself.

The analysis of the transference, that is, the projections of the past relationship with the parent introjected on to the therapist, enabled Ciro to use the therapeutic relationship, first to project his fantasies of being criticised and persecuted (he thought I would kick him out of the group because he was cruel to the others), and then to experience the possibility of a reparative relationship in which he himself chose to follow the rules of the "new parent" as an integration and substitution of the crazy parent he had had in his childhood.

Lucia's case: how to build one's own prison

Lucia is a beautiful young woman aged thirty-four when I meet her for our first interview. She dresses like a man, she is a regular soldier and she asks me about psychotherapy because she feels unhappy about her private and sentimental life. She has lived for several years with a man she used to love, even though she has ambiguous feelings towards him. She has been trying to leave him for years, she says she can no longer make love with him, that she no longer feels sexual desire for him and she feels bored. At the beginning of their relationship there had been an abortion, because Lucia had become pregnant during the first months they had been dating, and she decided to interrupt her pregnancy as she wasn't sure about their relationship. Her companion had not participated in the decision, but she blamed him for not reassuring her or encouraging her to keep the baby.

Lucia was, in fact, desperate when she thought back to the abortion; she said she had always wanted to have a baby and that he had not understood anything about her. After the abortion, they had started living together, but she had become more distant in the relationship with him, and she had never been able to have sex serenely after that experience. Even at first, they didn't have sex very often, but later on her difficulties increased and their intimacy had fallen apart, both on a physical and an emotional level. They no longer talked to each other or had fun together. During therapy, I find out that Lucia's is a traditional family. Her father is a soldier, too, her mother is a housewife, and Lucia is sure that they would have thought ill of her if they had known about the abortion. She has extremely old-fashioned beliefs about sex, she is afraid that her father considers her a "whore" because she has had more than one boyfriend, and she is ashamed of being beautiful—which she disguises in her camouflage clothing. In individual therapy, Lucia cries a lot when I tell her that she has built her own prison herself and that a life sentence as a punishment both for her and for her companion is deeply unjust. During group therapy, Lucia re-examines her past, succeeds in separating from her companion, with whom she can share nothing except fraternal affection, and lives alone for a time. She is serene and she learns to enjoy daily life again, begins to laugh and have fun again, dress up, have female friends, and go on holiday. Then, she finally falls in love and ends therapy. She comes to see me the following year; she holds a baby and hers is the radiant and satisfied face of a happy mother.

Key concepts for TA psychotherapy

The ego state model, the concept of script, transactions, and games are the four basic concepts which enable a quick diagnosis and facilitate the situation of the patient within a diagnostic frame of reference. They are also the concepts on which one is able to develop a plan of therapeutic intervention.

When we define the ego state as "a consistent pattern of feelings and emotions directly related to a corresponding consistent pattern of behaviour" we also provide the patient with a simple explanation about what he or she is experiencing and how it works.

At the very first meeting, I usually draw a scheme on the whiteboard, with which I can graphically represent the distress the patient is experiencing and explain that if the connection between thoughts, emotions, and behaviours is appropriately related to external reality, a person can find the resources to face what he or she is going through. However, if there is distorted thinking (for instance, if I'm before my boss and I think he is a bear who can eat me up), the emotions I feel will be related to the sense of danger which has been activated inside me. I might therefore act by avoiding certain behaviours and sometimes even by flatly refusing to go to work.

Another scheme I show my patients is the functional tripartition of ego states, since with a simple scheme, many of the conflicts discussed in the first meeting can be explained. When a patient declares "If I take a day off, I feel guilty", this derives from an internal dialogue of which he is unaware and which in therapy can be explained as a conflict between his Controlling Parent and Adapted Child. In particular, it is as if the Controlling Parent were saying: "In order to gain my appreciation and esteem, you have to work" or "Don't waste time" and the Child feels adequate only by sticking to these rules or living up to these expectations; hence when the patient allows himself a day off, he pays for it by having a guilty conscience.

Such beliefs come from the introjection of parental messages, perhaps coming from the real father (who never took a day off and was proud of that), and contrast with the compromise decision taken by the Child ego state. As a result, the patient does take a day off, but then it is ruined by a sense of guilt.

In this case, the Adult is not able to mediate the conflict deriving from the efforts of the Adapted Child—who wishes to obtain approval: "I want to be admired and act like you"—and the need to rest and have fun coming from the Free Child. So, if the Adult acts according to the Free Child's needs and takes a reasonably deserved day off, the conflict remains unresolved, as it is impossible to satisfy the internal Parent.

Transactions are explained as both intrapsychic and interpersonal dialogue, and the logic schemes of the dialogue make the complex world of interpersonal communication comprehensible. Crossed transactions are explained as transactions that break off a relational sequence that either we or the other person decide to end. They are, therefore, helpful to individuate both our and the other's position in the exchange and to obtain the desired change.

When we want to stop dependence, or even a symbiotic scheme, the best thing is crossing communication. For patients who are beginning psychotherapy, it is very motivating to find out that some little things can be changed very rapidly, even just the annoying and bothersome talks with our colleague in the office, or the usual conflict with our former spouse or adolescent son. The issue of ulterior transactions leads to the concept of psychological games and to the observation of typical games which represent the relational manifestation of the script.

"If it weren't for you" or "Look how hard I've tried" are games described by Berne long ago, in 1964, and they are still quite typical games nowadays; they are commonly experienced and talked about in the first therapy sessions. It is very good for the therapist to recognise them and know how to deal with them. We certainly know that at the beginning of therapy it is necessary to play the games of the patients a little, because crossing a transaction right away would make the "contaminated patient" feel scolded, and he could not accept it, thus deciding not to come back again.

The patient's script starts to become clear thanks to both the ego states diagnosis and the games described by the patient and played with the therapist. However, it is fundamental to add a careful listening of the patient's personal history as it is related in the first sessions (later on, the interaction with the therapist will change the narration).

This way we can draw a script matrix which represents the transactional analytic diagnosis for that patient. From the script matrix, and the psychiatric diagnosis, and the psychodynamic diagnosis from the *Psychoanalytic Diagnostic Manual* (PDM Task Force, 2006) with reference to the attachment model, we have what we need in order to establish a therapeutic plan.

In order to plan a therapeutic intervention, the therapist must be able to correctly listen to the patient's uneasiness, make a good diagnosis, and have the tools necessary to think about and create the plan agreed on with the patient. A TA therapist can plan psychotherapy in accordance with the schemes of the ego states diagnosis and the script matrix. She can thus talk about the work to be done with the patient, explaining it in language that is comprehensible for any adolescent or adult who is in the office, whatever his level of education.

It is reason for pride in TA that technical language is made simple in order for the patient to understand it.

The objectives of therapy

Berne wrote in 1966:

> In practice, the whole transactional theory of personality—the effects of early experiences, decisions, positions and their consequences, the Santa Claus fantasy, the collection of trading stamps, and the value of metaphor and humor—are summarized in the transactional-analytic position "I'm Ok, you're Ok", expressed in the following language: Every human being is born a prince or a princess; early experiences convince some that they are frogs, and the rest of the pathological development follows from this. [...] In these terms, there are two therapeutic goals. The first tries for something called getting better, or "progress", which in effect is making more comfortable frogs; the second aims at getting well, or "cure", which means to cast off the frog skin and take up once more the

interrupted development of the prince or princess. Transactional Analysis aims for the latter. [...]

The patients learn from bitter experience that "progress" is not enough, that the only thing that will give permanent and satisfactory results is to get well, which means getting back their memberships in the human race. (Berne, 1966, pp. 289–290)

Getting well means thus to rediscover one's potential, take up once more the interrupted development, find a balance with the environment which lets one feel spontaneous in relating to the world. Ciro, the patient described above, says: "I've reached my highest level in the healing process" when he is about to leave the group, feeling satisfied with the life he has created for himself and that he can lead.

Therapeutic tools with TA

In his latest book, Michele Novellino (2012) talks about a therapist's toolbox. A TA therapist actually has a great number of tools, which are not systematised in a single manual. The TA therapist's technique implies a refined art of restructuring the patient's talk through a dialogue of simple therapeutic operations, described by Berne himself (1966) in the famous book on group therapy that I quoted above. According to these operations, the therapist leads the patient to reorganise his discourse—and thus his mental disorder—in a new logical order and emotional balance. A transactional analyst is an expert in language and emotions. She cannot merely read them, but uses them to rid the patient of his contradictions and the ominous influences of past messages and pathological introjections, and then leads the patient to develop linear thinking and deeper emotions. This will later enable the patient to choose what he really wants to be and how he actually feels, to rediscover—as we will later see with Gabbard (2000)—"his or her real Self". Above all, a psychodynamic transactional analyst knows that the main tool in the work she builds, in interweaving dialogues with the patient, is the analysis of the therapeutic relationship. This indeed creates the conditions—through the building of a specific and carefully managed setting—for the processes of transference to re-enact, here and now, the archaic conflicts to be modified and solved.

CHAPTER THREE

The setting

W hen we talk about setting in psychotherapy or counselling, we mean all those procedures that define the nature of the therapist–patient relationship.

The setting is made up by the rules that help to build a relational environment that is technically suitable for the therapeutic relationship. The relational environment is constituted of both the setting (environment, room where meetings take place) and the administrative, ethical, professional, relational agreements which define the relationship between the two people who meet for a session.

Set and space

The environment where psychotherapy takes place must have a silent, reserved, welcoming space designed exclusively for the interview or for the group, if treatment requires it. It is therefore fundamental that the study where psychotherapy and counselling take place are designed specifically for it, and that colours, furniture, and room arrangement are thought out for the specific purpose. This means that in TA you never use a desk (neither the psychotherapist nor the counsellor sits behind a table), as it would represent a barrier between the client and the practitioner. We want to be in the Adult position and meet another Adult before us, that is, we must be in an equal position with the client.

The TA therapist usually works in a private centre, and it is inadvisable to wear a uniform or a doctor's gown. It is recommended to wear sober clothes that, nonetheless, describe the therapist's personal style.

It's like saying: this office and my clothes define me; here I have my music, my colours, but you can have your own space on the scene. Indeed, if sounds, perfumes, music, or colours are too intense, it is as if they do not allow space for the other, so that he cannot be with us as a protagonist, only as a spectator.

A psychotherapist's office is not the stage for an actor who recites monologues before the spectator-client: on the contrary, it can be a stage where one can find a protagonist role and interact with a person who listens to us and creates a space for the other person to express himself.

So, when a therapist chooses furniture for her room, it is advisable to ask herself: will I be comfortable in this place? And will my clients be comfortable and have their own space to feel like protagonists in this room?

Nowadays, there are competent professionals who can help us choose appropriate lights and colours to create a welcoming environment. Indeed, for someone who starts working as a psychotherapist or counsellor, professional advice is as important as consultancy is for those who design a personal web space or business card.

If we decide to have music in the waiting room, or magazines to be read, even these details need careful thought, so as to create the opportunity for a positive first impression which should not prove too obtrusive for the client.

The environment must also provide, and guarantee, privacy. When working in partnership with other practitioners or in counselling and psychotherapy centres, the administration office's task is to welcome patients with due respect. Rarely does this happen in health clinics or medical consulting rooms, which often prove to be less patient-friendly environments, unsuitable for our work. Nowadays, clients and patients of psychotherapy and counselling are no longer uncomfortable if they have to wait in a waiting room with other people. Nonetheless, it is always preferable to set precise appointments and not have the patient wait.

Time and duration of sessions

Arranging a precise appointment and having the patient enter the room right away can be a therapist's choice. However, another technical choice may be to have the client wait for some minutes in the waiting room, or to leave him or her alone in the office for a few minutes. Thus, the client can concentrate, and some can also take a break from their hectic pace.

A saying of the Andean Indios goes: "Now, I'll sit and wait, because my life has dropped behind"; the time of the meeting is intended as a pause in the hustle and bustle of everyday life.

If one feels that the session must be something to be over with quickly, arrives hurriedly, speaks frantically, and hastily runs away in order to do something else, one may lose the benefit and the opportunity of the experience that is being lived, just as eating compulsively prevents us from tasting the food we are eating. Therapists and counsellors thus have to be aware that it is necessary to provide an occasion to slow down the pace, think and feel emotions—which cannot happen in a frantic ride.

Precise timing and duration of sessions, usually between forty-five and fifty minutes, define the time of the professional performance for a psychotherapy interview.

If a practitioner does not respect the time framework, she is not able to provide limits for either the anxiety or the narcissistic omnipotence of her own, as well as the patient's, Child part. Getting used to respecting the times we agreed on is very healthy for the patient, and only a precise time framework enables the therapist to observe a great variety of behaviours in the patient in terms of respect of rules and limits. Some people end a session before time by checking their watches (as if he or she were over-activated in his or her Parent or Adapted Child ego state); some speak very quickly so as to be able to say as many things as possible when the time is about to run out (greedy Child) and some even continue talking when the session is over, as they are being accompanied to the door or while the invoice is being filled out (vicious, morbid, and almighty Child).

Others deliberately reveal their secret just a couple of minutes before the end of the session so as not to feel ashamed or to avoid the risk of intimacy, which is felt as too invasive. If the therapist makes the session longer, she does not respect the client's choice to "drop the bomb" and discuss this issue the following week. If possible, it is helpful to organise a treatment plan, giving a weekly rhythm to the meetings, possibly at the same time and on the same day. This rate, and the stability of the meeting, greatly facilitate clients and patients, as well as the practitioners who can dispose themselves to meet that particular person, review their notes, or listen to a recording, thus focusing on the person they are going to meet. When a therapist does not even know who she is going to meet in the following hour, she is too stressed out and close to burn-out; such a condition should be considered as a sign of a problem to be dealt with, rather than a normal rhythm of work. Therapists must also have mental space and time to think about their patients. This helps them to establish how many people they are actually able to follow.

Payment

The cost of the session, including the price of the first interview, must be clear for a new client. It proves helpful to communicate our fee in the first telephone call, when a client calls to arrange the first appointment, in order to avoid unpleasant difficulties when he arrives. A colleague of mine had to have a discussion with a new client at the end of the first session because the client expected not to pay for the first interview, as he claimed that he had already had two interviews with other therapists and he had had them for free. A quarrel at the very first meeting can prove useful for a diagnosis. However, it's unpleasant to deal with such a problem at the end of the session with very little time left. It is necessary to suggest an administrative contract, as it is called in TA, that is, a bilateral commitment in which the practitioner explains her fee, payment mode, and rules in case the patient skips the appointment (the order of the psychologist's price list gives the possibility of deciding whether to reduce the fee for a cancelled appointment, ask for it anyway, or waive it).

If our setting comprises weekly sessions, and the therapist reserves that time for that particular patient every week, it is actually correct to ask for the entire fee anyway. In some cases, one can accept that the session is cancelled if the therapist is informed by a time previously agreed on. As for group therapy, it is correct to ask for a fixed fee for every session, even from those who do not attend, because the economic commitment is no different from a subscription. When setting up the contract, the therapist must establish the rules for holidays and breaks during the year. Of course, it will not be possible to foresee every single case. It is therefore very helpful to examine with the Adult the confrontation with the problems that may arise from this. Questions of money and payment often give rise to relational games and further levels of challenge, provoking aggressiveness. There is always the patient who will ask to be "saved" by the therapist and claim not to have enough money to pay for the therapy, perhaps after wasting their money by gambling or on cocaine. The therapist who falls into this trap and accepts the ploy for a salvation game will end up destroying the possibility to really help that patient and confirm the game "Let's pull a fast one on Joey". That potentiates the sense of narcissistic triumph of the antisocial person or the patient who aggressively punishes the therapist, robbing her of her fee, and discounting therapy in which he will not commit to changing his life. It may happen that a patient who is usually very reliable, at a certain phase of therapy, suddenly starts "forgetting" his wallet and cannot pay for the session. This is, in effect, material to be analysed, a psychological aspect to be taken into consideration in the analysis of the transference relationship. It is probably even more relevant than what we are discussing during the session, especially if the event occurs more than once. As a matter of fact, some patients, at some point in the course of therapy, say that they are sorry that the relationship with the therapist is only on a professional level, that they are worried that the therapist does not care for them and is interested only in their money. As a consequence, they may unconsciously try to carry out some tests to understand whether they will be sent away or will be allowed to continue the therapy. A therapist and a counsellor can handle with balance, and as Integrated Adult, the issues of setting and payment if they have previously laid down their life experiences and discussed in supervision sessions their possible difficulties. Those who are embarrassed if they have to issue a receipt, ask to be paid, or remind a forgetful client of the contractual agreement, need to turn to a supervisor to analyse the countertransference problems about such questions. Otherwise, they will miss a great opportunity for psychological work with their patients. During therapy, everything that happens deserves to be observed, taken into consideration, and analysed, in order to verify whether the event is connected with the problem brought to the session.

What to tell the patient about therapy and method

There is always a whiteboard in a transactional analyst's office, so that she can give information to patients and clients about the method and the language that is being used. It is thus helpful to give some simple information about TA, counselling, or psychotherapy, and the language one is going to share with the client. It does not mean delivering a lesson, but providing examples about the method, for instance, giving feedback to the client through either the ego state model or the analysis of games and transactions. A transactional analyst must be proud of using simple language, comprehensible to everyone, even adolescents, which does not require specific education. Human behaviour must be explainable and understandable for every client. If a therapist considers that the client cannot understand her explanations, psychotherapy is probably inappropriate for that client, as psychotherapy is dialogic therapy, whose main tool is the word—and therefore language. It can be helpful to give the basic information during two or three sessions, without providing the client with too much information all at once. In the first meetings, the patient, especially if he has arrived with a burden of feelings of anxiety and anguish, does not want to listen, is only anxious to get rid of his inner emotional load and will not therefore be able to understand a long explanation of theory.

Making a contract

TA method is intrinsically contractual and is therefore contractual in psychotherapy as well. This means that client and practitioner "as adults who sit and talk" define together the problem and the objective—or rather the objectives—which they aim at attaining, having examined the obstacles and resistances that might come up. Making a contract on objectives to accomplish is not an easy operation; it actually requires a significant amount of decontamination. Some people come to therapy but their expectations are not realistic. "I don't want to be depressed ever again, or suffer from mood swings" might be a magical expectation of a bipolar patient, who will have to change this expectation into: "I want to learn to accept my mood swings, get cured and lead a healthy life. I want to accept that I have to take medicines to help me live my life." This means making one's own biological instability a condition to cope with, which can be controlled through prevention, a healthy rhythm of life, and perhaps permanent pharmacological treatments, just as diabetics, or anyone who suffers from metabolic disorders compensated with medicines, do.

We currently know that some medicines can save your life, and a competent psychotherapist can play a very important role in accompanying a patient with immature and grandiose thoughts to acquire a more balanced and realistic attitude.

Another unacceptable request is to change another person. Each one of us can determinedly struggle to change ourselves, if we ever can; indeed, we, as therapists, cannot accept that someone comes to us because they want to change somebody else without being willing to question their own assumptions and their relationship with the other person. The request to change another person may be, for example: "I'll come to couple therapy so my husband can change, as he would otherwise never come to individual therapy." This is not acceptable, because couple therapy affects both members of a couple. If one of them considers himself or herself immutable and blames the other for the problems, it is impossible for a therapist to work under these conditions. Similarly, no one can guarantee that "If I do therapy, I'll become more self-confident and I'll reconquer my husband", because we never know what is going to happen: a system changes its balance as one of its members changes. What this woman wishes may actually happen, but the couple is more likely to break up completely when one of them reaches a psychological position of greater self-confidence. Acceptable contracts are those which comprise realistic objectives and the analysis of the path to be followed in order to reach them. "Doctor, will you make me feel well? You are my last hope." "The result depends on the work we will do together."

In some cases, the therapeutic contract must comprise a Parental kind of intervention; these are the cases in which the therapist creates a protection for the patient. This is always required with patients suffering from serious eating disorders, psychotic patients, bipolar patients, people with suicidal tendencies, and drug addicts. In such cases, the patient must accept the basic conditions so we can accept to plan his treatment. The patient must agree to be followed by a psychiatrist for pharmacological treatment, to attend a centre for drug addiction and have toxicological checkups, and to sign a form which allows the therapist to alert someone from the family if she thinks the patient's life is at risk. These agreements are comprised in what in TA is called a "no suicide contract", which can be roughly formulated like this: "I'm willing to help you if you give information about your health, and together we will do everything we can to keep you alive, including the possibility, for me, to inform someone from your family and your doctor if I know you're in serious danger."

How long therapy lasts and when it ends

In preliminary interviews, it is helpful to talk about the duration of counselling and therapy. Counselling is always a short-term intervention, whose aim is to solve a specific problem and enhance the client's awareness; it is important that it is a clear intervention and not a disguised kind of therapy.

The same clarity is required in psychotherapy. The initial request may change, and lead to new and different contracts, but such changes must be made explicit and agreed upon together with the patient. A symptomatic TA therapy, aimed at obtaining the social control of the symptom, to use Berne's words, can last from six months to two years.

Psychotherapy, whose goal is to analyse the script and de-confuse the Child, that is, to restructure the personality at a deep level, actually lasts from three to five years, as it is an emotively long path whose length is determined by the physiological time required for learning and restructuring the script. I can determine average times thanks to my experience. In certain cases, you never know how long therapy will be, but it surely cannot last forever and it is rarely appropriate to continue it for a very long period. Attending psychotherapy for more than five years is justified in situations characterised by significant frailty, in which the therapist takes on a supportive role, almost like a "parent" substitute. These, however, are very delicate situations, which it is helpful to discuss with one's supervisor, to be certain that, from a clinical point of view, continuing the therapy is appropriate.

The efficacy of the intervention and its duration are elements to be evaluated both by the professional and by the client-patient; close to the end, exchanging opinions on the goals achieved and on how and when to stop is always a very stimulating and enriching moment.

Some people reach an impasse when the practitioner says: "Well, it's time to think of a closure contract. When will you be ready to leave?" Experience indicates suggesting three sessions for completing the work done. This means that in the first contract the therapist must ask the client to agree to discuss the interruption and the end of the intervention. Such an agreement prevents "acting-outs" or the patient suddenly disappearing without there being the chance to give him some feedback or a healthy way of saying goodbye. Indeed, clients and patients must be granted the right to leave if they feel they are not being helped or cured. They have the right to keep on being an alert Adult and decide what is best for their health; it is healthy not to trust those therapists who interpret any interruption of therapy as an acting out of the patient, without ever questioning their own assumptions. For some patients, a healthy path begins when they have the nerve to quit unsuccessful therapies, just as for some sons or daughters, life begins when they leave their parents' house.

Can you reach the therapist outside of the session?

Every therapist and counsellor usually has precise agreements about these aspects too. However, while contacting counselling clients does not create major problems, and each individual case can be defined and discussed every time, the question is more delicate with patients in psychotherapy. The psychoanalytic roots of studies on the setting have contributed to generating assumptions and dogmas on this issue, which have often given rise to prejudices and strictness, particularly in young therapists.

Any contact between patient and therapist must indeed be oriented to the contractual objectives on which their relationship is based, and the nature of their dialogues must, accordingly, be completely professional. A therapist is neither a support line nor a rescuer; she is a practitioner who can be reached at specific times (the patient must know the practitioner's telephone availability) and in particular circumstances agreed upon by patient and therapist. A therapist can decide to be reached by email or by telephone, but it must be clear if and when she is going to answer. It is better not to reply to mail or text messages, unless one has to reschedule a session.

Every time we deal with personal issues, we must do it in person in a session, where the transactions can be directly observed. A patient tells a therapist: "If you want to know me, read my blog", thus showing the desire to go beyond the limits of the session, a need to show off, and voraciously eat up and invade the therapist's mind. It is important not to accept such proposals and to define the time we will dedicate to the patient within the boundaries of a contractual agreement. Outside of the session the time dedicated to a patient is, for a therapist, time spent thinking about him during supervision or in clinical study carried out in order to be really helpful to him. Accepting the narcissistic system by reading his books, chatting in blogs, watching his drama performances or artistic representations, is not appropriate. To the patient who writes, acts, or paints we can say: Choose something of yourself we can read or see together here.

Problems in setting

When I began working as a psychotherapist, like many young people, I wasn't comfortable meeting people who were much older than me. I was afraid they would not take me seriously because I was "younger". In Italy, in particular, wisdom is considered to be the domain of the elderly, so it is very difficult for a young therapist to be recognised as authoritative and competent. I remember that one day I was waiting for my first interview with a patient of my psychiatrist colleague. He was being treated by her pharmacologically for a serious bipolar disorder. The story of this man was long: his first psychiatrist had left with the patient's wife, and he tended not to trust other people and to feel betrayed. When the time of our appointment comes, he enters, followed by another man, who is introduced as a taxi-driver, and the patient tells me: "Dear doctor, here is my taxi-driver friend; you should pay him, because I haven't got any money on me." So, I rapidly think, not only doesn't he have the money for the session, but he even wants my money to pay for his taxi-ride, and I immediately get annoyed. I then decide to ask him if he has his cheque-book on him, and when he answers that he does, I ask him to pay for the taxi with a cheque, and then to come to therapy. After I have overcome this obstacle, I feel better, and I understand I have passed a test. For the moment, it is not easy to pull a fast one on me, and I haven't let him discredit me. However, I had to be very careful not to let him turn our meetings into a magnificent show, which would suddenly have been interrupted as soon as he experienced a depressive phase.

CHAPTER FOUR

The clinical interview

Choosing a therapist and the first contact

When a person decides to go to a psychotherapist, either to begin therapy or for consultancy, he has to face the problem of *choosing*. He thus starts looking for a competent practitioner and "the right person". Some people rely on the opinion of relatives or friends, of their doctor, while others evaluate different options by analysing information and references on the Internet or in books and magazines. This research itself provides helpful information about how the future patient functions. As a matter of fact, it is as interesting as exploring that person's knowledge of psychotherapy, fantasies, and expectations about what will happen during a psychotherapy session as well as the assumptions, prejudices, and rules that are associated with a correct psychotherapeutic setting. In TA terms, it is interesting to know how the internal Parent (assumptions, judgements, and prejudices, protective strategies or lack of protection that have been activated during the research) led that person to us, how, and how strongly, the Child affected this process (fantasies, archaic emotions, magic expectations, over-adaptation to being referred by someone else) of deciding to come to us. Besides, was the decision taken in accordance with an operative Adult with appropriate information, procedures, and realistic expectations? Such initial conditions can be explored during the first meetings, and this will provide us with precious information about the personality of the person before us.

There is always a pre-constituted transference which is completely independent from our own person, and indeed it is given by the personality—we say the script—of our patient. These data are not immediately accessible to the therapist, and can be revealed by the patient only if a therapeutic alliance, solid enough to set up a contract and establish a fairly stable relationship, is built up. The way our first contact happens, however, provides us with precious and immediate information. Nowadays, therapists can be reached in several ways: a phone call at the office or on her mobile phone or by email. When a therapist is contacted through a medical centre or psychotherapy centre, where the contact is dealt with by a secretary, the person who answers the call may be asked several things. It is important that the person who takes the first message keeps it, and tells the therapist who will conduct the first meeting what the initial request was. For example, a woman's voice, without introducing herself at all, asks the secretary of our counselling and psychotherapy Centre: "I have been advised to undertake some TA therapy, and they tell me I need a male therapist, but I don't know … is there someone who knows TA in your centre?"

In the sentence of the client/patient there is no subject, and someone who advised/referred the woman is implicitly mentioned, indicated by the word "they". The person who takes the call doesn't know who the referring person is. However, he or she can guess that, before the request, an exchange of opinions with someone, or some kind of reflection, has taken place, and this person must have provided indications, suggestions, advice, at least in three different fields: psychotherapy as a cure, a definite psychotherapy field (which indicates that the person is competent in this field) and even an evaluation about the gender of the therapist (to indicate, perhaps, a pre-comprehension of a problem concerning the male/female or father/mother relationship). Besides, such a confused request for a meeting indicates that this person has some difficulties in saying specifically who she wants to talk to. She is unsure and very anxious, and her request is not Adult-defined: she is asking for information, she wants to arrange an intake interview, she is obeying somebody's instructions and is making an attempt without a real desire to meet a therapist. It is, indeed, a first attempt to overcome the fear of this meeting, and the voice of the person who answers this call, as well as how clear the reply is, will either encourage or discourage her in continuing her exploration. For this reason, it is fundamental that a psychotherapist personally answers the phone at pre-established times (that she is therefore reachable) or has a competent secretary, prepared to deal with first contacts and give valid information. A secretary of a medical office is not usually helpful in this first contact.

Counselling, a basic prerequisite for psychotherapy, begins when we give information about books, magazines, awareness campaigns about health, radio or TV programmes, blogs and Internet sites, and when you have the first contacts with people who may later become clients and patients. A request for an appointment can be formulated in several ways, which we can examine from a point of view either of the words chosen or of the non-verbal expression, according to the ego states.

Prevailing Adult ego state:
"This is XY, I would like to fix an appointment with you."
"Can we fix an appointment?"
"I am a patient of doctor X's, and I would like to undertake psychotherapy. Can you meet me?"

Ego state of Adapted Child influenced by a Critical Parent:
"Well ... I don't know, I think I need to have a talk with you."
"My wife thinks I should start therapy."
"Do I really have to tell you my name?"

Ego state of Adapted Child (I play "Gee, you're wonderful, Professor", according to Berne):
"Doctor, finally I can talk to you! If only you knew how many people talked to me about you! They told me: talk to her, she is the only one who can help you."
"I've been told you're extremely good!"

Ego state of Rebel Child (Adapted vs dependent):
"I have already tried different therapies but they proved unsuccessful. Do you think you're up to the task?"
Provoking: you can't make it with me—"hatchet man".
Challenge: let's see if you can succeed where others have failed (I'm doing xy therapy, but it doesn't work).

Triangulations, or more than one person during the first contact

Sometimes the person who calls is not the one who wants to undertake therapy: it can be his wife, or her husband, or a parent. More frequently, it is a woman who phones, with the patient next to her.

In these cases, I suggest letting me speak to the person for whom the appointment is being requested, without criticising the person who is calling: this, too, is data to collect, information we receive. I choose to accept appointments made by a different person, a wife or a parent. Then, I discuss with the patient the way the contact took place, without criticisms. I consider it very important for the therapist to be friendly, and never to confront the person before meeting him. Telling someone: "Tell the patient himself to call me", especially if the tone is critical or can be perceived as brisk, can be a transactional crossing and implicit criticism both of the person who called and of the one who is behind the scenes. Similarly, when more than one person shows up for the first interview, I greet everyone, and then I ask who I have to speak to. In an interesting case of a forty-year-old man, the appointment was made by his wife. On the phone, she added that her husband would be accompanied to the meeting by another woman, his lover, with whom she had an agreement about this. An interesting piece of information: the two women of this man had decided that he had to start psychotherapy, and this beginning is a precious element both for diagnosis (an Over-Adapted Child, a probable personality disorder) and to understand the system of transactional games in which the three people are involved. I will later get to know that when the two women had found out that this man was living two parallel lives, the man had threatened to commit suicide because he did not want to lose either of them.

Referral

It is helpful to know who referred the patient. Sometimes, the patient gives this information in the first phone call: "XY told me to come to you". Otherwise, it is helpful to ask during the first meeting: "How did you decide to come to me?" If the answer is: "I looked on the Internet or in the Yellow Pages", it can be helpful to analyse what made our patient choose our name or profile among many others. If the answer is: "Doctor X sent me here", our relationship with this doctor may be a relevant element to be considered. If Doctor X is someone who knows and esteems us, the fact that he referred a patient to us indicates our professional competence is being recognised. On the other hand, if Doctor X is a person with whom we have a conflictual relationship or whose envy we are afraid of, this referral might be an element to be worried about. We can suspect that the patient is a problem, a "hatchet man" as psychotherapists say, that is, an impossible patient who starts therapy only in order to show that nothing, or no one, can help him. Some therapists always consider it a gift if a colleague refers a patient to them, whereas others tend to be suspicious, and see it as a "time bomb". Indeed, it is important to be an Adult and accept the referral, and decontaminate our perception in order not to be either ingenuous or paranoid. Right or wrong, we are actually influenced by the referring person.

The first meeting, at last

It's the day of the appointment, and finally the meeting between two people who might start a therapeutic or counselling path takes place. It is helpful to observe whether the client arrives early (it could indicate a high level of anxiety, a very Adapted Child, an influencing Critical Parent), if he is punctual (Adult control and/or obsessive traits), if he gets lost (confusion and conflict), if he arrives very late (oppositional traits, prevailing Child). Then, at the time arranged (being on time is very important: you show respect for the other person and you also collect diagnostic elements about the patient—you do not confuse data with a possible pathology), you walk towards the person you are waiting for and let him into your office. You introduce yourself with a smile and a few sober words, then invite him to sit down while you do the same. In a transactional analyst's office there are always at least a couple of armchairs, a whiteboard to write on, and sober furniture which reflects the therapist's style. It never contains extreme colours or pieces of furniture which might offend the patient's sensibilities.

I watch the person who is sitting opposite me. How does he present himself?

Does he smile and look at my face or keep his eyes down? When he enters, does he rub against the wall and bump against the door, enter with his head held high or bowed? Does he ask where to sit, take up as much room as possible or as little as possible? Everything about this meeting is important and meaningful. Our mind and our senses are activated. The same happens to the other person. I observe the way he is dressed, the sensations evoked at an analogical level. I smell nice or bad smells, I listen, I shake his hand.

And what about the new client? Is he observing me, studying me? Or does he seem not to see me and keep on with his internal dialogue? Is he acting on a stage where the lights do not let him see the audience's faces? Does he ask where to sit or does he autonomously decide? Does he start talking or does he wait for me to begin and ask something?

The therapist should soberly introduce herself and then let the client say his line and take the stage. For example: "Good morning, I'm doctor Z. Please talk to me. I'm listening."

Berne said that in therapy there are two adults speaking. I cannot add much to that because this is already a lot. Everything happens in this face-to-face meeting in which a whole life, a personal story as well as deep emotions, are summarised.

Words, music, images are a whole, and cannot be separated. The major issue in our profession consists in developing our capacity to listen and to feel deeply and in sincerely being willing to meet the other person. We have to be capable of welcoming the other person and guiding the unveiling of the mystery he embodies. If we perceive the other person only as an "object", if he is rendered banal or fully described by his diagnosis, or by the first request he makes, the therapist misses the opportunity for deep listening, and thus for a meeting with the *person*, that special individual who enters our room that day. As long as we keep alive our curiosity and interest in the meeting with the other person, we protect therapeutic potential, which is generative and curative due to its being a mirror for the other, who can see himself and rediscover both the joy of life and a good guide to unraveling the troubled confusion that each one of us has gone through in life. A therapist is a positive parental figure capable of guidance and nurture, a qualified adult, competent at analysing the human mind; a child who is still capable of being surprised and is sincerely interested in meeting another person.

Listening

When I am with a patient, I listen to his sighing, or crying, while I am observing a long silence, a look, a flexible, stiff, neglected, or disguised body. And I also listen to the words: either clear or confused narration, interrupted, with words not completely uttered, or a flow of words. The narration takes place on at least two levels:

The problem, the story that brought me here today and the request I make (first level);

What I cause to happen in the here and now of the meeting in terms of revealing myself and relational questions (second level).

Nelly's case

She tells the therapist she has just met: "A friend of mine studies psychology. She told me that I should see a therapist because I often have obsessions, I fight with my boyfriend all the time, and he will eventually break up with me. She says I have problems with men, and I should see a male therapist ... I think it's because of my father. He was never there, while mum was always there for me.

I'm twenty-three, I was a flight attendant but now I'm an English teacher ... I have a relationship with X, but he told me that he will leave if I don't seek therapy because he can't stand me any longer. I'm obsessed with passwords, I must know all of his passwords. I call him all the time when he's at work to know if he has changed them, I have to repeat them to myself or I feel bad, terribly bad. I know it's not normal. I end up ruining every sentimental relationship. I want to do something to feel better. I can't take it anymore, either."

As she talks, she gives me information about herself on a nonverbal level too, and this is even more explicit than her words. Nelly often winces and twitches, especially when she starts telling about her affective area. She nervously bursts out laughing when she says that others cannot stand her anymore. Her tone of voice when she talks about herself (Adult aspect) is different from when she directly asks me a question (Child aspect): her voice is suddenly whiny and broken, and she seems not to be able to pronounce the words properly.

The here and now of the meeting represents an important unveiling.

Nelly does not mention her twitching, faltering, or suddenly changing her voice, her making faces, as if all these elements were not in themselves telling something about her at this meeting. There is a tale within the tale, and it represents the most relevant part of the meeting, as this is the part that has to be interpreted. The Child ego state of the person before me is enacting the deep relational question, what she is really asking me as a therapist, what she is asking me and revealing about herself in spite of her Adult, and probably behind her inner Parent's back, as if the Child secretly were giving you a sheet of paper with her secrets on it. The patient thus lets the deepest core of her self express itself, and discreetly reveals to the therapist who she really is, what drama, unresolved issues, conflict, or void terrorises her. In Nelly's case, it is surprising that she does not mention her heavy twitching, although some minutes after she begins talking, this strongly affects her discourse, becoming a tale within the tale. I finally ask: "How long have you had nervous tics?" Nelly's voice changes (she goes back to being a detached Adult and her nervous tics disappear) and she tells the story of her family. She starts twitching again when she uses emotional expressions to convey the information which she otherwise gives without interruption. Nelly says that her nervous tics started when she was about six, that they tried to cure her with Haloperidol. It was too heavy for her, so she gave up medicines. Her parents separated when she was ten, and she went to live in Scotland with her mother. Her father is Italian, and until then they had been living together in Italy. "He never wanted me, I went to him in the summer and he didn't want to be with me, and I came to live here, so, I thought, he won't be able to escape." And yet Nelly says that her mother was there for her, took care of her. Nelly's behaviour, however, shows insecurity and instability, which indicates things are not so simple. I insist, and I ask again about her mother: finally, Nelly tells me that her mother was epileptic but had stopped taking medication, and that she had seen her mother have a terrible epileptic crisis when she was six. Then she says that her mother has a new lover in Scotland, that he is depressed and that his dog pees on Nelly's mother's pillow. Nelly has a father who avoids her, and her mother is anxious, epileptic, ambivalent, and neurotic (Nelly says: "There must be a reason if the dog keeps peeing only on *her* pillow!").

She says she has got used to thinking about her twitching as something not to cure, even though I find out that when she was in school she was labeled handicapped and called an idiot for this reason, and that she actually suffered deeply because of it. She does not mention how her twitching can cause her problems in her job as a flight attendant, or as a teacher. I ask her, and she says that when she works, she can control herself. She asks me if I can help her be less anxious and controlling.

Her obsessive-compulsive disorder is ruining her relationship with her boyfriend. She calls him dozens of times a day when he is at work, just to know if he has changed the passwords in his computer, and she cannot get any rest until he tells her the passwords and reassures her. Now, he is threatening to leave her if she does not seek therapy. Nelly concentrates only on her obsession about the passwords and on the idea that sooner or later everybody will abandon her.

Objectives of the first meeting

Starting to know the person I meet (A-A and C-C).

Making a person who experiences some kind of distress feel welcome (P-C).

Listening to the question and the problem (A-A).

Laying foundations for therapeutic alliance (P-C).

Giving information about the process of counseling or therapy (A-A).

The first interview

It can be helpful to encourage the patient to describe the reason why he has come to see us with a statement, such as: "Talk to me. I'm listening" (in a friendly tone of voice and Adult attitude) and then ask an open question, such as: "Do you want to tell me something about yourself?" (with the hint of a smile, and being willing to listen). If the therapist usually takes notes, she has to tell the patient why she does, and ask for the patient's consent. Explaining the confidentiality of the setting, and what professional confidentiality is, is always useful. As the patient narrates, the therapist can ask questions when the patient pauses, or when he is clearly not capable of going on autonomously. When the Adult prevails, and we can proceed because an alliance has been established, questions can be asked for greater specification or clarification, but without exaggerating: you cannot expect to get all the information at the first meeting. When a therapist is at the beginning of her career, it is not easy to decide the right timing and how many questions she can ask. It is important to keep in mind that there are two people involved in the meeting: a hurried pace makes you feel pressed, whereas a slow pace and a very silent therapist can make the patient feel he has been left alone. Some practical rules can help the therapist understand when she should stop:

The patient answers a direct question with a redefinition;

The patient cannot find the right words, is anguished and gets easily frightened;

The pace of the conversation is too pressing, and seems like an interrogation.

At moments like these, giving reassuring feedback, which reveals how the therapist has actually noticed the difficulty in the patient or his avoiding attitude, can be really helpful. For example, you can say: "If we begin psychotherapy, we will get back to this, we will talk about it in the future."

Paying attention to ego states observed during the interview is crucial for a TA therapist. In fact, they represent the interweaving connection of the patient's whole personal history and the story expressed by the micro-sequences we can observe in the meeting. The description of the problem and the anamnesis are usually confirmed by precise relational signs given by the patient to the therapist, who knows how to read them. These are phenomenological manifestations of archaic ego states. Such ego states are usually revealed in the present time of the first interview. When you can film the interview and watch it together with the patient, he is often surprised by certain photograms depicting a face that shows contempt for his parents, or sarcastic laughter, or a defiant attitude which only apparently is not consistent with what is being told. A technique of microanalysis of videos, which I have been using with those patients of mine who consent to this, comprises watching parts of the interview together with the patient and commenting together on what we see. I found it relevant to have the patient act as a co-therapist in re-analysing the interview.

First of all, the patient's narration in the interview

In the clinical interview, if the patient can express himself through free and uninterrupted narration, the therapist is provided with interesting elements, as the narrative structure of the tale reveals more about the patient's script. The focus of our interest is how this story is told, where it starts, where it goes, if the patient is the protagonist or has a token role, which actors and characters are chosen to be mentioned and which others are hidden. A counselling client of one of my colleagues does not mention in his story his two-year old son, with whom he lives; in his narration, he focuses only on the conflict with the woman he is involved with. When the counsellor explicitly asks how he would define his relationship with his son, he answers: "I didn't mention him because I'm not here for him, my problem has nothing to do with him".

The fact that this patient does not mention his son in his narration, nor have him in his mind, will be interesting food for thought, both for my diagnosis and in order to outline a treatment plan. I can hardly imagine how one can ignore the presence of a two-year-old child who lives in the same house! For a script therapist, it is helpful to know about Propp's structural analysis of fairy tales (1958) and the structuring of narrative thought. In fact, this is as important as knowing the interview and medical anamnesis grids, and it is fundamental to getting used to accepting the first spontaneous tale and, only later, asking questions to integrate this narration.

The interview is helpful for the anamnesis

Preparing an anamnestic grid to be filled in with the information given by the patient can be helpful at the beginning of therapy. Clearly, collecting data is not as important as starting a therapeutic relationship, as the latter comprises an exchange based on trust on a non-verbal level—and therefore on an ulterior psychological plan—and the chance to listen to a spontaneous narrative text. In a therapist's file there will be room for the spontaneous narration as well as some elements for an interview grid to be filled in, not necessarily within the first three meetings:

> Name, age
> Geographical and cultural place of origin
> Current and/or previous occupation
> Education
> Marital status and with whom the patient is currently living
> Children? If they do have children, what's their age?
> Health conditions and physical illness
> Relevant accidents
> Current or past psychic illness
> Current problem that brought them here

> Members of the family of origin
> Family history of psychic illness
> Relationship with food and alcohol
> Relationship with smoking and drugs
> Experiences of addiction and relationship with money
> Possible sleeping disorders
> Relationship with sex
> Interests and hobbies.

In addition, it can be helpful to ask what the patient knows about therapy and TA and what he wants to know about me (reciprocity helps to establish the contractual process).

From the first interview to the therapeutic contract

TA therapists often suggest to the person they meet for the first time, a brief experience of exploration so to decide whether to undertake psychotherapy. In my experience, I find it helpful to suggest two more meetings after the first, thus having three meetings to define the therapeutic contract or carry out a first consultation, which can end simply with a restitution to the patient of an evaluation of the problem he brought. The first three meetings precede the therapeutic contract and are necessary to move from the initial request to the agreement which TA therapists call "contract". These meetings are necessary to define the possibility to undertake therapy, to define an initial framework for the setting, and enable a micro experience of psychological treatment. There, we agree on when we are going to meet, the duration of the meetings, the fee, our policy about telephone calls, skipping a meeting, and privacy. The initial request is analysed, and we eventually make an agreement on how we will proceed if psychotherapy is proposed as a tool for the analysis of the problem and as a cure. At the first meetings, the recurring questions from patients are:

> "Am I going to heal?"
> "How many sessions will it take to solve my problem?"
> "When do you think it's going to end? I can't afford to feel like this for years!"
> "Are three meetings enough?"

Every question is legitimate, and therapists have to remember that psychotherapy is not very well known as a tool for analysis and cure, and fears and prejudices about it are widespread and common. You therefore must answer these questions, and a therapist's answers have to be:

SINCERE: the duration of therapy is variable.
ADULT: I will give you all the information you need, and we will decide together how to proceed.
EMPATHIC: I understand that you can no longer stand feeling so bad.

The therapeutic contract is the objective one is going to achieve, and it comprises the agreement on how we are going to work together in order to attain this goal.

Describing the setting to a patient in the first interviews

Giving the patient information about therapy and setting in the first meetings helps to make an Adult contract later on. I have already said that it is important to be clear about the aspects of the administrative agreement, an agreement on the objectives and methods of therapy, as well as an agreement about the therapist–patient relationship: I have to maintain professional confidentiality and give you professional support; we will not go out together or have a relationship outside the context of the setting; you can tell me that you want to go on with therapy or give it up whenever you want.

Psychotherapy is dialogic, it is developed through interviews and, sometimes, through the group. It requires payment and the payment can be invoiced as a health service. Meetings are weekly, or anyway take place regularly, and last forty-five to fifty minutes. That their duration is precise must be communicated to the patient and respected by the therapist, as the attitude of both the therapist and the patient to the given time limit is relevant. There are people who reveal a secret at the door while they are about to leave: others tend to go beyond the limits and take up the next patient's time, thus being inconsiderate towards the other patients—and sometimes in the same breath as they are saying: "I wouldn't want to encroach on your time, you will certainly have other patients!" Some other people peer at their watches as they cannot wait for the meeting to end, and feel protected by time passing. A person's attitude to time actually reveals a lot about the internal and external transactional space, about what happens in the spatio-temporal microcosm of the session concerning the way he imagines and projects his occupying time and space. Does this person invade the surrounding space or slip as an invisible presence through possible meetings, trying to "leave no trace", as Delia said, with a very thin voice and presence. The world is a theatre set on to which we are thrown, Heidegger would say, and on which we live within the limits of our birth and death. I believe that, if we observe and break the clinical interview down into sequences, we can have a presentation of the comedy or tragedy, just as in a cinematic trailer.

CHAPTER FIVE

Contractual treatment

T A psychotherapy is a contractual treatment. This is one of the first things you learn as a trainee. What exactly does a patient-therapist contract mean?

Social contract between therapist and patient

There is obviously an administrative kind of agreement between the two people: I will be coming to your office for psychotherapy sessions and I'm paying you a fee, just as in any other private professional service. This is the kind of agreement we have with a lawyer or a chartered accountant. The professional offers a service of consulting or therapy and we consider her qualified for that and, as clients, pay what is due according to precise tables and fees.

This agreement, which comprises an exchange between adults socially defined in accordance with shared regulations, was summarised by Claude Steiner (1974) in four points:

Mutual consent: an explicit agreement on goals and objectives of treatment (we decide that this will be a dialogic therapy, composed of a number of psychological sessions within a time frame that has already been established or will be determined during the therapy itself, and such sessions are oriented towards the accomplishment of a shared goal).

Valid consideration: the nature of the relationship will be professional; this implies that the patient will be paying for therapy and that behaviour on both parts will be professional, in accordance with a system of explicit rules both for the patient and the therapist (accordingly, there will be a fee, professional confidentiality will be maintained, and the relationship will be defined within the rules of the setting clearly made explicit to the patient).

Competence: the therapist offers her technical competence in her knowledge of the mind and those psychic mechanisms which cause the disorder, as well as techniques to treat it. The patient offers his Adult capacity to co-operate in the *treatment path* (a psychotherapeutic cure cannot work unless the patient co-operates, is willing to reveal himself and to create an alliance with the therapist. At the same time, in a perspective of correctness, a therapist's commitment is to use her specific competences, and turn to a supervisor or the scientific community if a case should prove too complex. The therapist's competence is a scientific and professional competence (A) and therefore demonstrable and comparable; it is not magic (interaction P—C) or due to personal qualities, as may happen with non-professional and untrained people who act as healers).

Legal object: the therapeutic objective and the ways to accomplish it must be socially and legally consented (the TA therapist clearly explains to the patient the deontological and ethical aspects she follows).

In the first meeting between therapist and client (I say *person* when he calls, *client* when he comes for the first time for consulting, *patient* only after we have defined an agreement about the cure and, therefore, clinical acceptance of him as a patient) the therapist absolutely must dedicate at least a few minutes of the session to explaining how psychotherapy works, what rules the setting comprises, what specific competences she will offer, and what is required from the patient in terms of behaviour and payment. For some therapists, myself included, the first interview is actually made up of three sessions, in order for the therapeutic contract to be defined. This is an appropriate amount of time both to give the person who might become a patient some feedback about the problems he brings us and to give the other person a chance to see our method of intervention. I find it very helpful, at these sessions, to reanalyse the problem the patient brought us in terms of ego states described on the whiteboard or sometimes with a metaphor corresponding to the primary image I have intuitively created about the patient.

Lucio's case

A forty-nine-year-old man comes for a first meeting. A colleague of mine, a psychiatrist who has been treating him for two years for an anxiety disorder, has referred him to me. My colleague advised him to undertake psychotherapy, as his response to pharmacological treatment is low. Besides, he suffers from strong anxiety and a constant state of depression because of his lifestyle. Lucio tells me that he began suffering from anxiety and depression as a child, when he was about six. He thinks this was due to the fact that he was left alone for hours, since his parents were in business and worked the entire day in their own firm. Lucio was brought to a specialist who suggested the child should take up sport. Lucio remembers he felt better when he began playing in a football team. After giving me this indication about a very far-off time, he adds that as a grown-up he was well until he was forty. He got married early, had two children, and started his own business. He kept playing football until he was thirty-two, and he only quit to follow his first son when he played at a competitive level—similar to what Lucio had done. However, he adds, since he turned forty he has had alternating periods of slight depression—which were, however, very heavy periods due to a constant state of anxiety, low sexual desire, and a low tendency to pleasure in general—and serene periods, in which he felt that things were under control. He has been working with his father for the last five years ("My father works tirelessly and he is very demanding and efficient"), and this has increased Lucio's anxiety ("On the other hand, he's not so young, and I couldn't leave him alone. I have also thought that maybe he will finally appreciate me, that I have a chance to show him what I'm worth!"). He adds that since he started working with his father, he hasn't been able to have normal holidays, as he worries about his father. Lucio is afraid that his father will work too hard if he is not with him. His wife is very angry though, because they no longer have moments of intimacy and pleasure as a couple. And yet, he says: "I don't want to lose her, it's just that I can't feel well or strong enough to take a break from work."

At the end of the intake interview, I propose this analysis: "You see, in your internal dialogue, your Parent is even more of a Stakhanovite than your real father, and an inner voice tells you: 'You can't quit, you have to try hard and show him you can work as well as he does. Can't you see that he is eighty and still he keeps working, he never takes a vacation?!' You have learned to correspond to this model and try hard to demonstrate that you live up to your parents' expectations. Lucio the child could play football only because it was a cure—'Doctor told me to'. Similarly, now, being ill is maybe a way to obtain permission to change something in your pace of life and work. 'You have no right to play or dodge responsibilities other than for cure!'"

Lucio smiles and says: "That must be it. So, when can I come back?"

This is a little example of the language and the method I use to make the patient more aware about choosing psychotherapy. It also helped Lucio agree on the fact that he cannot be well until his Child identifies other ways to escape the pressure of Parental expectations, which today comprise a set of interiorised beliefs and ideas which often make him feel inadequate, too weak to be really OK.

Contracting

Transactional Analysis originated as a group therapy, and Berne's first and most relevant considerations about the contract are in *Principles of Group Treatment*, published in 1966. A TA group is a contractual group in which both the therapist and the patients "start off, with the unprejudiced attitude of a man from Mars, and try to evolve out of the actual realities of the situation a contract which is acceptable to both sides". Berne offers us an interesting example of an alcoholic who tells the therapist: "I want to give up drinking". The therapist asks him "Why?" After listening to the patient's reasons, the therapist says: "These are not your reasons. These are other people's reasons. Why do you want to stop?" If the other can accept this objectivity, you can make a good contract from the very beginning of therapy. Otherwise, both patient and therapist can clearly explain what situation the patient is in—he does not have his own motivation to start therapy. The therapist can decide to accept the patient as long as he is aware that if he is not personally motivated, therapy will not be effective. A contractual form of therapy is a kind of relationship based on equality—I'm OK-you're OK—which makes the patient responsible and clarifies at each phase how each participant can contribute to solving the problem. Each person, even someone who is suffering a lot, is capable of taking a little responsibility for himself. Indeed, they have taken responsibility to undertake therapy. The patient's freedom and his responsibility in therapy imply that, on the one hand, the therapist is Adult in her attitude, and explains her interventions. On the other hand, the therapist must allow the patient to be critical and sceptical, and sometimes even accept that he does not trust the therapist or is lying to her.

Sometimes people say: "You know, I don't believe in doctors or psychologists, and I don't even think that someone can help me with my problems. I agreed to come and talk to you only because my wife insisted a lot". I always reply: "Well, nobody can ask you to believe in something you don't know. I consider it wise of you to decide yourself whether psychotherapy can help you. I will explain how it works and I will show you the method in our first interview, so that you can understand and decide if I can be of any help. I ask you to help me understand why you have been advised to see a therapist and what your difficulties are. You are free to decide what to tell me, or to tell me very little, and I will give you my opinion on what you decide to show me or tell me about yourself."

Berne writes:

> The advantage [...] is that both of them are clear as to how they will know when they are accomplishing something. [...] In some cases the criterion may be a quantitative one, such as a lowering of diastolic blood pressure or increased earnings by a gambler or salesman; in still others it may be the relief of a physical symptom such as impotence or a specific phobia; or a change in behavior, such as not beating the children, refraining from taking alcohol or drugs, keeping a job, passing examinations, or finding a respectable girlfriend. (Berne, 1966, pp. 88–89)

Timing

> Since the therapeutic contract is usually a long-term one, there need be no hurry in setting it up, and ample time can be taken to explore its possibilities both in individual interviews and in the group; then on some auspicious occasion its terms can be agreed upon. (Berne, 1966, p. 93)

If the person who comes to therapy is very confused, it may be important to dedicate some time to setting up the contract, and explaining the reasons why you will proceed step by step, rather than setting up a contract between an Adapted Child and a Controlling Parent. In order to set up a contract, the agreement on objectives and how to achieve them must be established between the Adult ego-state of the patient and the therapist, thus implying a process of decontamination in the patient. That is to say, being able to make an effective contract is already itself part of the therapeutic process, and it therefore cannot be strictly considered a starting point or a prerequisite. It is very helpful for a therapist to keep in mind the social and behavioural diagnosis of ego states. If the other person is in the Child ego state or has a very Child- or Parent-contaminated Adult, his competence to define a contract will be faulty, and the therapist might risk establishing an alliance with pathological parts of the patient.

Sometimes, accepting a goal suggested by the patient is just a tactical choice. However, it requires an expert therapist to be aware that the contract will have to be reformulated as the patient acquires greater knowledge.

For example, Giulio asks the therapist to be freed from anxiety, and cannot identify what this anxiety indicates about his psychic functioning, how he could learn to read it and use it as a message. If a therapist said: "Learn to keep your anxiety and understand what it means", the patient would run away because he would feel he is not being understood in his suffering, from which he wants to be relieved. Indeed, when you feel bad, you look for immediate relief and you only want to feel better, rather than to understand. It is better to accept that Giulio comes to therapy to free himself from the anxiety that blocks him and does not let him have a normal professional life. However, you have to explain that although controlling his anxiety can be achieved in a short time if he activates his Adult, such a goal might be rediscussed together if the disturbing anxiety should prove to indicate a necessity for deeper changes in the intrapsychic and interpersonal system in which Giulio lives. That is to say: OK, we'll lower your fever so you can feel better, but we'll also have to understand what it's due to; if infection is developing, we must identify it and cure it in order for you to heal, that is, to find a long-term solution.

The psychological level of the contract

The contractual process between therapist and patient involves all the ego states. Indeed, in order for it to be effective, the agreement must address the Parent with its system of rules and beliefs introjected from real parents. The Child ego state, however, must bring to bear its energy and emotional availability. It is the Adult ego state that chooses and decides, but if one does not involve all the different inner voices, the agreement will be sabotaged and will not lead to anything effective. The psychological level of the contract is the implicit level where negotiation between ego states—and thus the different parts that come into play in the therapeutic relationship—either agree or are in conflict, mediate or avoid each other. The implicit level is thus the exchange of transactions which takes place on a level which is not completely conscious: smells and subliminal perceptions are involved as well as looks, and these elements evoke and define the possibility to find in the other person either the reparative parent or the one who will confirm his script, the partner for a repetitive game or the teacher who can guide him to learn how to feel better in his life. In therapy, it is mainly the patient who chooses on this implicit level, while the difficult task of the therapist consists in decoding the ulterior level quickly enough to understand how this script level can be used with the patient.

If a patient begins therapy to understand himself, but on an implicit level wants to show that no one is as good as him and that he will be gratified temporarily by the very narcissistic dominion over the other— "Even therapists aren't as intelligent as me"—the therapist might waste a lot of time searching for the reasons behind the repeated attacks on therapy, if the implicit level of the game proposal coming from the patient is not clarified. There can be a moment, in the course of therapy, when renegotiating the contract is advisable, starting from the explanation on such a level: "Well, since you are probably more intelligent than me and have just proven that, how can this discovery help you? And how can *I* help you?"

Patients choose the "right" therapist to follow and cure them when they feel ready. Otherwise, they choose a therapist with whom to play their script when they are not yet ready to make a real change. Sometimes, it is surprising to observe the superficial and apparently incongruous way they choose the therapist, even agreeing to work with someone they did not like from the very beginning, or someone they probably considered incompetent. Such choices, apparently making so little sense, might, on the contrary, have unconscious psychological motivations, just like those which, according to Berne, make us play games. Let's see if this is a "Joey", if I find someone I can seduce, or if I can demonstrate that no one can beat me; let's look for someone who becomes my step-parent and rescues me. Similarly, therapists can have ulterior motives for their therapeutic work, motives which are not professionally determined but script-determined: finding maidens to rescue from the dragon, killing dragons to satisfy bloodthirsty queens or kings, finding spectators for a theatre that is by now empty, satisfying a maternal or paternal need to be stroked by someone who depends on you and has a worshiping and uncritical attitude. Let's say that there can be narcissistic motivations, sadistic satisfactions, and much more, along with a healthy wish to help someone by offering one's professional competence in return for money. Only good psychotherapy and a constant personal and professional growth through supervision and professional updating can enable therapists to provide the tools to identify and keep under control their own instincts and archaic parental or childish levels. In this sense, a competent and honest therapist knows that a long therapeutic course is like a journey, and that it requires constant monitoring, because the levels of transactions involved are deep and the emotional intensity of the things exchanged is not always so easy to identify.

What then does a patient do on a psychological level with the therapist? He plays his script, giving the therapist a chance to add to the game fundamental variations that may, in turn, enable the patient to learn less destructive and challenging games in order to obtain love, strokes, and recognition.

What does the therapist do on a psychological level with the patient? She shows she can listen, is patient and willing to be there, involved on all levels, with her smell, senses, intelligence, and heart, so as to offer the patient a warm and sufficiently protective environment where she can rewrite the patient's intrapsychic system, so that it will become a friendlier world both for himself and others.

Phases of therapeutic contract

Making therapy contractual thus means making explicit what is implicit, and negotiating with the patient's Adult the steps he has to take in order to achieve the change he desires. As therapy proceeds, the contractual approach consists in describing the process to the patient. A contractual frame of mind is acquired by patients as well; if they are actually involved in a process of personal growth, they will be able, and required, to evaluate what is happening from their own point of view, and later to exchange views with the therapist to decide together whether they are getting any advantage from therapy, and how. "It is one thing to make a commitment and to begin operations under it, another to carry it through to its stated goal. As operational ratification proceeds [...], either the therapist or the patient may want to make amendments, and these can be frankly discussed" (Berne, 1966, p. 96).

Patients have a right to be confused at the beginning of therapy, and this may happen again at critical moments of the process of change, when dark, undistinguished visions bringing about moments of discouragement or angry depression—"You are abandoning me and I still feel so bad!"—come about. The therapist must be clear and continue along the path, helping the patient to go forward even through such misty visions.

> The fact that the therapist and patient set up operational criteria for improvement does not mean that the ultimate goal is merely the alleviation of symptoms or the attainment of control over social responses. It only means that such changes will be taken as definitive signs of improvement and as gauges of the effectiveness of the treatment. The therapist will always be on the lookout for the determinants underlying the symptoms or responses. This means that the contract will have to be amended from time to time. For example, if the therapist has in mind first the alleviation of symptoms and secondly the investigation of archaic attitudes towards parental figures, he may keep the second part of his plan in reserve until an appropriate time, and then propose it as an amendment to the contract. (Berne, 1966, pp. 90–91)

Group contract

> The patient's side of the contract [...] is only that he will from time to time offer the therapist's consideration samples of his behavior towards other people. [...] The therapist's side of the contract is that whenever he thinks of anything to say that might be helpful to the patient, he will say it. (Berne, 1966, p. 92)

In this chapter of his book, Berne does not explicitly talk about the contract among the patients entering the group. According to what we said earlier, it comprises, on their side, to be willing to interact with others, observe and be observed, give and receive feedback, and maintain professional confidentiality out of respect for the other members of the group. A group setting is particularly stimulating because the interpersonal dimensions of the script (games and transactions) can be observed in action. This offers more elements than in the dual setting, where the same phenomena take place in the relationship between therapist and patient, with the aspects of transactional exchange caused by the here-and-now of transference and countertransference. In the group, a greater number of dynamics can be observed and acted out, and this indeed offers a great opportunity.

Closing contract

The end of therapy is a very precious moment, and it represents a crucial phase of the path itself. We can compare it to the end of our adolescence, or the moment we left our parents' house. In my groups, we always discuss the end of therapy contract, which means making explicit how and when a patient wants to end therapy in accordance with what the therapist and the rest of the group think. For most patients, this moment of contractual definition represents a significant step of redecision in which rapidly, over a very brief period of time, a new process of decontamination and deconfusion takes place again, in sequences that can be codified and observed. Some people are actually afraid they will start feeling bad again if they leave the paternal and maternal house represented by psychotherapy, once their path is concluded. In fact, they have already introjected the internal therapist, who acts as a Parent, and are actually autonomous, but they are not ready to admit it. Thinking you have to part, ghosts and shadows from the past emerge: will I be like Dante's Ulysses who goes past the Pillars of Hercules? For some patients, being physically close to the therapist, and the place of therapy, is like being close to an energy or water supply. Such patients aspire to interminable therapy, which would be a financial benefit for the psychotherapist but a terrible waste of time and money for the patient. Making a good end-of-therapy contract means exploring how the patient feels about leaving his home. This particular separation often means, for both, accepting to structure this period as one in which the patient relearns to separate from someone but nonetheless carry with him the energy generator. Sailing out to sea, we should have a small generator, solar panels, and desalinator, as well as a fishing rod. These are the instruments therapy must provide the patient with. Indeed, not everyone wants to leave for a trip on the ocean. Some people like to sail near the coast, and others like to live on their boat moored on the river or the lake. What is really important is that each one of us knows where we are and has the proper tools to go where we want to, or are able to, go.

Evaluating the therapeutic path

A good evaluation can be done only after therapy has ended, so it is very helpful to invite patients to a follow-up after six months, and then after one and three years, whenever possible. When this opportunity is created, we receive, as therapists, useful information about how certain processes of change have brought about different choices and balances.

CHAPTER SIX

Basic techniques: therapeutic operations

Frustra fit per plura quod potest fieri per pauciora (Ockham's razor)

In *Principles of Group Treatment*, Berne describes the intervention a therapist makes in conducting group sessions or interviews which aim at the change she wishes to achieve. "Taking as the most general statement that psychiatric patients are confused, the goal of psychotherapy then becomes to resolve that confusion in a well-planned way by a series of analytic and synthetic operations" (Berne, 1966, p. 213). In Chapter Ten, Berne briefly describes, with brilliant logic, how a transactional analyst conducts the dialogue in order to attain decontamination and deconfusion. Therapeutic operations are thus specific transactional stimuli that the therapist proposes to the patient in order to get rid of his confusion and to be oriented in the world of his own impulses, chaos of emotions, and primordial passions; in short to go from chaos to cosmos. Berne does not describe, in this context, the preliminaries of the interview or the group which comprise the transactions of encouraging, invitation to speak, and creating the atmosphere, which he describes in the first chapters of the book (e.g., "Well, tell me what makes you think so", or "Tell me what made you decide to come here, tell me something about you").

Therapeutic operations are all the interventions and interpositions aiming at bringing about change during the interview or the group session. The intervention is an operation on material brought by the client, while with the interposition the counsellor or the therapist adds new material. Let's imagine meeting a patient who admits she has a problem of compulsive shopping. Let's try to examine how an effective interview might be conducted with this patient according to Berne's operations. Of course, the interventions described below are not intended to be a sequence of interventions in the same interview. On the contrary, some of these interventions cannot and must not be precocious. It is necessary to understand and respect the level of awareness of the patient, and the ego state activated in that moment, in order to decide whether one can proceed with interventions.

Interrogation

This is a question designed to receive an answer that, besides informing the therapist, invites the client's Adult to think and share material in the interview or in the group and that will later be used to work on the problem he has brought (e.g., "Do you know how much you spent on your clothes over the last month?"). The objective of interrogation is thus to make the contents explicit and straightforward.

> Do use interrogation when confident that the patient's Adult will respond.
>
> Do not use simple interrogation if it is likely that the patient's parent or Child will respond.
>
> Sometimes use interrogation [...] to find out how the patient will respond. (Berne, 1966, p. 234)

The problem with asking a patient questions is that you cannot be too detached and inquiring. If the frequency of questions and the pace of the interview are emotionally in tune with the patient, the therapist can enquire and hence know when it is time to ask and when to listen in silence.

Specification

This is a declaration on the part of the counsellor or the therapist, categorising certain information. It may be assentive, as in non-directive Rogerian therapy (e.g., "So, you have always wanted to buy expensive things") or informative (e.g., "That's more of the little girl in you"). The objective of specification is to fix in the client's, and the counsellor's, mind certain information so that it can be referred to later without denials. Specification thus enhances awareness in the client, making him more aware about what he is communicating to us and sometimes causes insights (discoveries, intuitive illuminations) precious for the client.

> *Do* use specifications when it is anticipated that the patient might later deny that he said or meant something [...].
>> *Do not* use specification if it will frighten the client's Child [...].
>> *Sometimes* use specification [...] to see how far you can go without frightening the client's Child. (Berne, 1966, p. 234)

Increasing patient awareness is the primary objective of specification. This operation enhances thinking and sharing the thinking co-constructed between therapist and patient.

Using specification during an interview is like identifying some relevant points on the map in order to find our way through a confused bundle of information. Having the patient involved in the reflection, which is possible thanks to simple and common language—like that used to describe ego states or to analyse transactions and games—is helpful in psychotherapy. It activates the patient's Adult and helps to lay foundations for that essential co-operation in therapy which we define as therapeutic alliance.

Confrontation

This is an intervention on the part of the counsellor or therapist who uses information previously received from the client to underline inconsistency emerging during the conversation. This might disconcert the client's Parent, Child, or contaminated Adult, and put the client in a difficult position if the intervention happens at the wrong moment. It is an Adult–Adult transaction (e.g., "You are telling me that the situation is under control, but earlier you said that you don't know how much money you have in your account. How can these two things coexist?").

The objective of confrontation is to energise the uncontaminated part of the client's Adult. A thoughtful silence, or laughter due to an insight, indicate that such an objective has been attained. It is, however, a manifestation of the activation of the Adult, finally free from contamination.

> *Do* use confrontation if the patient is [...] playing "Stupid" [...] or if you are genuinely convinced that he is incapable of tagging the inconsistency himself.
>
> *Do not* use confrontation when it makes you feel smarter than the patient [...].
>
> *Sometimes* use confrontation if the patient forces you to by playing a hard game of "Stupid", in order to find out why he so badly wanted you to do it.
>
> *Caveat*: do not confuse legitimate confrontation with a game of "Critique" "You tell me how you feel and I'll tell you what's wrong with your feelings". (Berne, 1966, p. 236)

Confrontation is a key-passage of the therapeutic session. It is not at all easy to set up confrontation on an A-A level: it is much easier to enter a judgemental dimension about inconsistencies in what the patient is saying/the patient's speech. What enables a therapist to set up confrontation at the right moment and use it as an opportunity for the patient—rather than as an operation of "unmasking the guilty" or scolding the patient as a parent—is a true non-judgemental attitude in the therapist's mind. If the therapist is sincerely interested in understanding and analysing the strange and apparently incomprehensible balance among thousands of contradictions, this constructive process can begin. From my direct experience, it is mostly the intuitive activation of the Little Professor (archaic nucleus of Adult ego state or Adult in the Child, called A1) in the therapist which enables the Adult meant as A2 (second level Adult, who can have second-order logical thought) to establish confrontation conducive to thinking, smiling, and perhaps even insight in the patient.

Explanation

This is an intervention on the part of the therapist or counsellor that strengthens, energises, decontaminates, and reorients the patient's Adult (e.g., "At the moment, you are playing 'Yes, but ...', so perhaps you don't really want the advice you are asking me for. A part of you does want to concentrate on therapy, but another one encounters many obstacles to setting up the next meeting", or "You have told me that after three months in which you had no money left in your account, you stopped going out and even paying for therapy and medicines to punish yourself. Can you see that when the Child takes over and becomes hyperactive, your Adult disappears and your internal Parent punishes you by deciding not to buy even something helpful for your health?").

The objective of explanation is to provide the Adult, free of contamination, with precious information and nourish it in order for the alliance to be strengthened. Berne says:

> *Do* use explanation at every opportunity when the patient has been properly prepared and his Adult is listening.
>
> *Do not* use explanation if the patient is still "Butting" (Yes, but, ...), "Cornering" [...] or "Trapping" [...].
>
> *Sometimes* use explanation if the patient is wavering between playing games and facing up [...].
>
> *Caveat*: make your explanations as concise as possible—one or two simple declarative sentences—or you may find yourself involved in a game of "Psychiatry—Transactional Type". (Berne, 1966, p. 237)

Therapists are often inclined to give long explanations, sometimes expressed in a language that is not comprehensible to patients. If one decides, especially after a successful confrontation, that giving an explanation is useful, the explanation must be brief in order for it to be effective. A therapist who speaks too much makes the patient passive, and this may give rise to games, as Berne clearly stated. Explaining what is happening is again an invitation to think, to give a name to experiences that are anguishing or hard to understand; it also helps to analyse experiences one has lived through, to start hoping that the most disturbing feelings and thoughts can at least be contained, and eventually to start hoping to change.

Illustration

This consists of an anecdote or an exemplification the counsellor or the therapist provides after a completely successful confrontation for the purpose of reinforcing the confrontation and softening its possible undesirable effects. It is an interposition, an attempt to interpose something between the patient's Adult and his other ego states in order to stabilise his Adult and make it more difficult for him to slide into Parent or Child activity (e.g., "It's as if inside you there were a father that locks the naughty child in his room, and the child jumps out of the window, stealing his parents' money and feeling very satisfied because he's tricked them").

The objective of illustration is to reinforce decontamination and obtain alliance with the Child, who receives permission to be freed from Parental restrictions and be creative.

> *Do* use illustration when you are sure that the patient's Adult is listening, that his expressive Child will hear you, that his Parent will not take over [...].
>
> *Do not* use illustration if you are talking to a self-righteous or literal Parent (as with many paranoids). [...] Do not use it to elevate your own self-esteem by showing how clever or poetic you are. Do not use it in an attempt to rectify an unsuccessful confrontation [...].
>
> *Sometimes* use illustration to indicate that solemnity is not a necessary condition for therapy [...].
>
> *Caveat*: Remember the theatrical rule: a comedian should never stay on stage too long. And for a therapist, or a counselor, it is better not to go at all than to fall flat. (Berne, 1966, pp. 239–240)

Metaphorical language is evocative, it activates the Child ego state, prevents Parental judgment and enables the therapist to deal with very delicate material with the due protections.

In his lesson about lightness, Calvino (1988) wrote that it is like approaching the monstrous Medusa walking backwards and holding a mirror that reflects the monster, just as Perseus did, so as not to be petrified. I find it very helpful to use archetypical images in therapy, for example, from Greek mythology, as they belong to the collective unconscious of western civilisation. Indeed, in every people, mythology expresses, through effective images and stories, the great archetypical conflictual issues. If people from different countries came to see us as therapists, we should study, just like an anthropologist, the myths and stories of the civilisation they belong to in order to help them solve their individual conflicts. These archetypical references sometimes emerge spontaneously, as they are part of the patient's consciousness, and it can be defined through the language of a work of literature, a film, or a song. Heroes and myths with whom we identify are always explored in the script anamnesis and are very effective images in approaching the patient's inner world, just like dreams and reveries.

Confirmation

This is the operation through which the counsellor or therapist reinforces the Adult functioning by revealing new material brought by the client after confrontation and illustration. It, too, is an interposition, an attempt to strengthen the ego state boundaries (e.g., "Even with me, in therapy, your Child pressed you not to respect our economic contract, and in the first sessions you have often forgotten the money to pay me"). The objective of confirmation is to consolidate the decontamination process by adding new material that logically demonstrates what we have already stated after the confrontation. The client's Child can deceive even the most prepared counsellor or therapist. Confirmation can thus be an interposition that reinforces the confrontation of incongruences and contributes towards unmasking the Child. Quoting from Berne:

> *Do* use confirmation if the patient's Adult is established strongly enough to prevent the Parent from using it against the Child, and the Child from using it against the counselor/therapist.
>
> *Do not* use confirmation if the original confrontation was unsuccessful, or if the patient is "Butting", "Cornering" or "Trapping" [...].
>
> *Sometimes* use confirmation tentatively to test the patient's reaction [...].
>
> *Caveat*: again watch out for a game of "Psychiatry—Transactional Type". (Berne, 1966, p. 241)

Confirmation accordingly consists in using experiences we have shared, often in the therapeutic setting, in order to enable the patient to connect and assemble what has been observed within the microcosm of therapy with what happens outside of it. According to such a view, the group setting is the most suitable setting to provide material for either confirmation or denial of hypotheses which have previously been formulated. The group gives us a chance to observe and analyse several social behaviours and interactions which we otherwise might only have imagined through the script distortion. Some patients accept confirmations and confrontations mainly from the others in the group, and mainly if they have a very conflictual and ambiguous transference towards the therapist and learn more easily in the group than in the individual setting. At this point, the patient is decontaminated, and the therapist can proceed and crystallise the situation. If the therapeutic contract allows the therapist to renegotiate with the patient how and whether to proceed, she can discuss with the patient whether to crystallise and conclude this path with the relief of symptoms and an improvement of relationships or to proceed to help the patient overcome confusion through psychodynamic interpretation.

Interpretation

This is an operation typical of psychotherapy, not to be carried out in counselling. Its purpose is to deconfuse the Child. In a therapy contract, the therapist can propose such an interpretation: "When you behave like that, being so naughty, and let your angry father punish you, you end up looking for a 'fairy godmother' who magically rescues you and takes care of your bills and debts. In your fantasy this is maybe what you expect from your wife and from me as a therapist, that we pay for you and unconditionally accept you." The purpose of interpretation is to proceed to an analysis of the script, and this happens through the decoding of the cryptic material brought by the pathological Child with his regressive needs and tyrannical demands. Quoting from Berne again:

> *Do* use interpretation where and when the patient's Adult is on your side, when you are not directly opposing the Parent, and when you are not asking too much sacrifice from the Child or arousing too much fear of Parental retaliation or desertion [...].
>
> *Do not* use interpretation when the patient's Adult is not in the executive position or is not properly prepared or is not on your

side; nor when it is your Parent or Child talking instead of your own Adult.

Sometimes use interpretation to test whether a patient is playing a game of "Psychiatry" [...]. An interpretation may also be employed as a last desperate resort in the hope that after the patient leaves therapy, perhaps long after, he may be able to stop warding it off and use it.

Caveat: In some cases, the therapist is more apt than the patient to intellectualize instead of using his intelligence. (Berne, 1966, p. 245)

Interpretation is the central part of the analytic intervention. In psychodynamic therapy it also comprises the analysis of the oneiric material and parapraxis, acting-ins (acted in the setting), and acting-outs (acted outside the setting). Again, it is up to the therapist to use her experience and knowledge to know when she can proceed with a patient on an interpretative level, when the Adult is allied, the Parent is not judgmental, and the Child is not too scared. Personally, I consider it difficult to interpret unless the internal Parent is at least partially restructured and the patient has partially interiorised the new Parent learned during therapy.

Crystallisation

This is a statement from the therapist or counsellor to the client's Adult when he is in a condition conducive to change (e.g., "So now you are in a position to stop playing 'Cops and Robbers' or 'Let's pull a fast one on Joey' and manage your salary yourself if you want to"). In an existential sense, the therapist brings the patient to a position to choose, to exercise an Adult option on his life, and, if some contents have emerged which require deconfusion, to choose whether or not to do it in order to overcome an impasse. Again, according to Berne:

Do use crystallization as soon as you are sure that not only the Adult, but also the Child and the Parent of the patient is properly prepared.

Do not use crystallization if the patient is showing renewed signs of somatic disease, or a sudden access of courage or depression leading him into obviously hazardous situations.

Sometimes use crystallization if he merely *threatens* to acquire a somatic disease or to expose himself to undue hazards [...].

Caveat: do not confuse a Child "resolution" from the patient with an Adult "decision" on his part. (Berne, 1966, p. 247)

Other interventions: made by the counsellor's or therapist's Parent

For Berne, Transactional Analysis requires the eight operations described above. He adds that in some cases it can be useful or even necessary to use different approaches, particularly with psychotic patients, with whom it is preferable that the therapist be a Parent rather than an Adult for quite long periods during the intervention.

Support: this basically consists in stroking. Its content is not relevant, what counts is that the patient feels he is being encouraged. However, it is advisable that the supporting messages are protective and permissive (e.g., "Come on, you can make it").

Reassurance: in this case, too, the tone of voice and the attitude are more important than the content, and it works mostly if the patient's Child feels unprotected (e.g., "It's good for you to do so").

Persuasion: this contains seductive elements (e.g., "Why don't you do it?"), and the therapist must be aware that she will have to face the consequences of the attempts to arouse in the other person a decision to seek a cure for himself.

Exhortation: (e.g., "You have to do it for your health").

Berne adds that there are techniques that are directed to the Child ego state, but also that one must be prepared if one wants to use them. He also adds that there is a "bull's eye" transaction in which there is a therapeutic effect on all the three ego states of the patient; he says that this is the ideal to be striven for.

The bull's eye transaction

The bull's eye transaction is a stimulus from the therapist that has an effect on the three ego states of the patient simultaneously. It is very effective, and it usually starts the moments of deeper change when a redecision and a permission are being prepared. "I understand how difficult it is for you to give up your usual certainties [establishing bond with the P], but you can safely try new paths [permission to the C] because today you are able to choose and protect yourself [recognition of mature A]." This message was proposed to Sara several times at the last phase of her psychotherapy.

Sara: from ugly duckling to swan

Sara, who is now forty years old, is fine, works as a healthcare assistant, and has a happy married life. Sara has had a hard life; her family context was very fragile. Her father could not maintain his family or himself, and her mother was like a child—she has been dreaming all her life that the lover who kept her in reserve would finally rescue her. When Sara is thirty, she begins to experience depressive episodes, quits her studies several times, does not work. She starts therapy with this passive attitude and she is asked to find a job so she can pay for the sessions. So she takes up a paid professional training course which she will complete brilliantly, and she will eventually find a steady job. At the end of her first psychotherapy, she travels around Italy to enter competitive entrance examinations for employment. However, when she is autonomous, the bipolar disorder she suffers from becomes evident, so she alternates periods of excitement and hyperactivity in which she loses weight and has chaotic and accelerated behaviours with periods of desperation and blocks to her actions. She is treated pharmacologically and achieves a certain emotional stability, but she is still suffering and restless. In those years, she will frequently have to take care of people in her family who have cancer: her uncle, who brought her up, her father, and then her grandmother. She takes care of all of them with great concern, but soon she finds herself alone with her mother and her boyfriend, who cannot fill the void in her life. She starts seeing a psychotherapist again when, soon after she has got married, at the age of thirty-two, she herself gets sick with cancer. During psychotherapy, she finds support to face the hardships due to treatment and diagnosis, and she decides to fight and overcome her illness. After a couple of years of intensive treatments, Sara achieves a substantial remission of the tumour, so she goes back to her normal life, with periodic check-ups. It is during this phase that she starts psychotherapy for the third time, and she will be in a psychotherapy group for two years. Her objective is to "learn to live and be well", as she herself says. As a matter of fact, Sara cannot enjoy life, go on holiday, manage her money, make good projects, enjoy friendship, or love and laugh. This period of psychotherapy is very helpful for her, and Sara will be declared clinically cured from her tumour and in remission from her bipolar disorder. She will stop pharmacological therapy in agreement with her psychiatrist and she will fully enjoy those simple and "normal" experiences she has hardly known about.

An example of an interview: the Tin Woman in search of a heart

Vera is a young woman; she is twenty-seven years old. She graduated in maths and got a PhD in informatics. She works in a firm, and decides to see a therapist, as she says she cannot establish emotional bonds with people. She feels cold and rigid, and she cannot have sex with her boyfriend. She suffers from obsessive-compulsive disorder, a "loveless" and "joyless" script. The following conversation happens after twenty sessions, and we are at the real core of the problem. Vera arrives, and she is very silent, she claims she has nothing to say. In terms of contamination of ego states, we might say that Vera has a double contamination, of the Adult by the Parent due to which she confuses prejudice with objective data, and of the Adult by the Child as she rationalises her phobic part about contact and intimacy; she uses defence mechanisms of isolation from the people she loves and of rationalisation. The avoiding attachment pattern is clear.

> T: "Last time I invited you to focus on what you feel, and you took this as an invitation to 'make an effort', 'try harder', as a parental message" (*specification*).
>
> VERA: "Yes, that's true."
>
> T: "Accordingly, your Child part (*ego states*) reacted by being even more inhibited, and actually you are now telling me that you have nothing to say" (*specification*).
>
> VERA: "Yes."
>
> T: "So, you are bringing the child Vera, who is blocked and becomes silent if she feels criticised and pushed where she can't or doesn't want to go. Now, your sense of being blocked is stronger." (*specification*)
>
> VERA: "When you say blocked, you mean about my feeling? About my emotions?"

T: "Yes, as if the pressure you felt from me had reinforced your conflict between 'You should' and 'You can't'. What is it, though, that you're feeling now?" (*interrogation*)

VERA: "I feel like I have to say: OK, it's true." (*redefinition and shift from feeling to thinking*)

T: "This is what you think. Do you think this analysis is true?" (*explanation*)

VERA: "I also feel like: I can only feel if I force myself to feel something."

T: "So, what have you felt?" (*interrogation*)

VERA: "Fear, and, yes, I know the 'Try hard' (*script driver*) belongs to me. What can I do without trying hard? It's the only way I can feel something, and now ...?"

T: "You seem lost." (*interpretation*)

VERA: "Yes, I'm afraid, I feel like someone who has lost her way, and has no reference points." (*the phobic part emerges without being rationalised; the metaphor of space in a visual person who has such a marked control on distances is effective, and the patient goes on with the theme of orientation-disorientation*)

T: "So, you are afraid of being lost." (*remark*)

VERA: "Perhaps it's not even fear ... it's more like I can't do in any other way, and so, yes, it is fear, but it's because I don't know any other way."

T: "What do you mean? What is it that you don't have?" (*interrogation*)

VERA: "I have no idea how I can even start to do it in another way. Maybe I haven't got information, I've got nothing ..." (*the Adult, more decontaminated, reflects on the self*)

T: "As you speak this way, I feel protective feelings about you (*self-disclosure*), you are so cute, as if you were from another planet and you were asking me: help me become an earthling (*illustration*). How can one make contact with you?"

VERA: (her eyes are full of tears and she looks the T. in the eye.) *Insight* (*Child and ego states free from contamination*)

T: "What happened? You have just felt an emotion. What emotion are you feeling?" (*interrogation*)

VERA: "I feel abnormal, and I don't know what to do to become normal." (*parental prejudice about normal/abnormal*)

T: "Well, as a matter of fact you *were* crying, so you are in touch with some kind of pain, or sadness." (*explanation*)

VERA: "Yes ..."

T: "You see, you can feel! (*confirmation*) This sadness, this pain, immediately emerged. Which word aroused it?" (*interrogation*)

VERA: "Maybe the word 'alien'. You said I seem to come from another planet and want to establish a contact with you." (*Adult ego state: awareness*)

T: "What did that evoke in you?" (*interrogation*)

VERA: "The fear of saying ... I can't establish a contact with the people around me ... and maybe fear of solitude ..." (*Adult ego state: awareness*)

T: "You see, Vera, what has just happened between us is actually a moment of true, intimate contact. I felt protective, and you revealed to me your suffering, and this sorrow isn't new for you, you have felt it more than once. So, what happened between you and me is the opposite of what we were saying: there *was* an emotional contact." (*explanation and confirmation*)

VERA: "It's true. Maybe because I gave myself permission to reveal that since it was too intense—I couldn't keep it inside." (*Adult ego state: awareness*)

T: "Thus, the experience we have just had is that you *can* establish a contact if you find the key. It is an experience that contrasts with your script, an experience of permission, and I know you can feel and communicate your emotions." (*crystallisation*)

In Transactional Analysis, the intervention described above can be defined as an intervention of decontamination and deconfusion. In fact, when the Adult is reactivated, thoughts can be distinguished from emotions thanks to decontamination, and the therapist can provide, through illustration (use of metaphorical language), material for interpretation. This will bring about an insight in the patient ("I feel like an alien, I'm distant from everyone and I'm afraid I will be alone forever)", expression of the pain, and change in the ego state. At that point, in a brief sequence of transactions, the therapist gives a message of permission which sounds like: "You can feel, and you have just done it, you have told me what you feel and you made me feel something too, we have had an intimate exchange." The patient undergoes an experience of *rechilding*, according to Clarke's definition (Clarkson & Fish, 1988), of *kairos* according to Stern's definition (Stern, 2004, pp. xv–xvi).

CHAPTER SEVEN

Transference, alliance, and the therapeutic relationship

The therapeutic relationship

The relationship between the person who asks for psychotherapy and the therapist is the central element in understanding why some therapies are successful and some prove ineffective. In several studies, some of which are very recent, the relationship turned out, for different methodologies, to be the common variable due to which such a complex process as psychotherapy proves either helpful or useless. There is, first of all, a relationship between two real people that takes place in the psychotherapy room, and for any human action it is true that the quality of the relationship created between two or more individuals determines the success or failure of any co-creation. If this is true when one starts up an enterprise, when one explains the functioning of a work-team or a meeting, for the co-operation among the members of a volleyball or football team, it is clear that it can be even more significant for the particular type of co-construction of sense and meaning that constitutes psychotherapy. In the psychotherapy room, for weeks and weeks the patient reveals his own story, suffering, and secrets to a stranger who listens and helps the person who is narrating put back together the puzzle of events, understand reasons and the value of scattered emotions, find new paths, and express out loud the thoughts which emerge from the confused maze, so as to finally take decisions and directions, to get out of the blocking crossroads that are sometimes encountered in life. The person each of us would want in such a delicate and important process must be someone we respect as a professional, whom we consider correct and neutral, non-judgemental, and able to be empathic and powerful in intuition, and who has perhaps experienced some psychological distress and has, hopefully, been able to overcome it. I think that every patient who chooses psychodynamic therapy can have similar wishes and expectations about the therapist. No therapist can satisfy the expectation of a model of perfection and balance from every point of view, but indeed there is a moral obligation for the therapist to be honest and competent at doing what she claims to be able to do, a commitment to being in a process of permanent supervision and training. The real relationship between two people must thus comprise those aspects that have already been defined using the language of contract.

Transference

While on a conscious level the relationship is A-A, the unconscious psychological level contains expectations of, and projections on to, the therapist of the magic figure who is supposed to fill the void and heal the narcissistic wounds in a person's life, just as sometimes people have the same expectations of a romantic idea of love: someone will save me and satisfy my needs, as if one was back in an imaginary childhood where life completely depended on another person. Transference, then, implies projecting these expectations about a parental figure on to the therapist. Specifically, one seeks in the therapist what one expects to receive from the parent who determined one's attachment pattern. For this reason, it is helpful that we, the therapist, be sober and as neutral as possible, in order to observe how the patient interprets and imagines us, even when we say or do nothing. Transference interactions are very helpful in order to acquire information about the attachment pattern and therefore about very important aspects of the patient's script. If we know how to read what happens, we can see in short transactional sequences what the patient has experienced and what he keeps searching for or fearing in the significant meetings of his life. When our face is serene and almost impassive, we may be told: "I know you think ill of me!" or "Why do you look at me as if you were about to scold me?"

or again "Why don't you think much of me?" Other times, it is even worse: "Why don't you want me?" or "Do we really have to pay to have someone listen to us?" Some patients often forget to pay the therapist; if this happens more than once, the therapist must confront the patient and enquire what such a manifest aggressive attitude towards the therapist may mean. For example, Delia (case described in Chapter Twelve), requested, in the interview, a follow-up, saying that paying for therapy disturbed her, as she expected to receive something for free from the therapist and was quite annoyed by the fact that she was being reminded that the nature of their relationship was professional. Delia interpreted it like this: "So, you only care about the money and not about me." The therapist, however, explained to Delia that she was interested in her as a person and actually fond of her, although their relationship had the characteristics of a professional framework. For Delia, it was important to acknowledge that, in every affective relationship, she demanded to receive, without any demand on her to be committed to reciprocity, since she felt she had to be compensated for the harm done to her by having been abandoned as a child. Transference experiences can prove quite challenging for a therapist, especially if she has a "rescuer" script, since she may be easily hooked into symbiotic games and collude with the archaic needs of the patient.

During the first phases of her treatment, Sara, the bipolar patient described in Chapter Six, filled up my analogical voicemail with messages in which she desperately asked for help and wanted to be called back. It was very difficult to negotiate a less invasive behaviour and try at the same time to understand what these repeated calls were caused by. In one lucid moment, she declared: "When I'm upset, I feel better if I even simply hear your recorded voice on your voicemail." So, we began working so that she could autonomously develop her own reassuring internal voice rather than go around begging for reassurance. While Sara was telling me: "In the past, nobody would listen to me when I was afraid", I thought that on the other hand it was not easy to put up with such voracity, and how hard it might have been for her mother to be close to her. When I describe Terry in Chapter Ten, we see how the transference themes, which we have finally been able to analyse in the group, enable her to understand the drama of her avoidant attachment and help me, as a therapist, to get closer to the little wild child I had caught a glimpse of behind the apparent ice woman shown on the outside.

Novellino (2004, p. 133) writes:

> The script is an unconscious plan of life, which belongs to the area of transference phenomena, since it represents a derivative of this, or better an adaptation of reactions and experiences of one's childhood, an attempt to repeat in derivative form a whole transference drama … An important clinical consequence is that an urgent motivation of the Child is to re-enact his script through the transactions acted with the therapist. By remaining independent from the patient's manoeuvres and properly carrying out his job to analyze resistances, instinctual vicissitudes and the transference, the therapist prevents being seduced.

The therapeutic alliance

The alliance is half-way between the real relationship and the analysis of transference, let us say. In TA, by alliance is meant the willingness on behalf of the Adult ego state of the patient to co-operate with therapy by providing the therapist with expert support in getting to know the person before her, as well as the opening of the Child ego state towards the person who may intuitively be helpful in the process of change, while the internal Parent, too, progressively removes the obstacles and the envy competition which might compromise everything. When I think of alliance with a patient, I often realise that gaining his trust is comparable to being accepted into a whole patriarchal family when one arrives as a stranger or a guest. At first, one is welcomed according to some social rituals, decided by the community in a standardised way, and examined by the adults. Then, the children go near the stranger, to play with and smell her. Only eventually do the elders, who have been observing from a distance, start a conversation that is decisive in understanding whether or not the stranger can be trusted. Something similar, in such a plural process, happens between the many internal voices of the patient and the therapist as a stranger who approaches the patient's tribe—or at least the reserved territory of his intra-psychic world.

The countertransference

Countertransference is nowadays described within the psychoanalytic community as all the emotional reactions of the therapist to the patient, and thus not only the therapist's projections on to the patient. Countertransference is thus not only the "mistakes" you make as a therapist with the patient, but, most generally, the emotions he evokes in you, which it is helpful to take into consideration. It is indeed true that sometimes it is the countertransference emotional reactions that become the *gimmick* for games in which the therapist is *hooked* by the patient. For example, if the therapist plays games in which he has the role of the rescuer, an unresolved problem in her is probably being acted, due to which she tries to be forgiven for archaic guilt or to finally receive the recognition deserved through "rescuing" actions. On the other hand, sometimes therapists act as persecutors and are judgemental with those who do not gratify their narcissistic needs, and tend to be critical and punishing towards patients who do not adapt. In supervision conducted with TA methodology, we often listen directly to recorded sessions and discuss with the therapist both the explicit transactional exchange and the implicit one, which is more easily understood from both voices. I have recently discussed with a colleague in supervision about how she was being critical of a patient of hers. My colleague told me that the patient tends to have two script drivers, "try hard" and "be perfect", and how this had given rise to several blocks when she was growing up: for example, she quit university. In a session we listened to together, the patient enthusiastically said she had faced a situation in a very different, unusual way for her: she had been assertive, she had had her rights respected and had been listened to. Paradoxically, for me as a neutral listener, the therapist started to investigate and criticise the "imperfect" aspects she had noticed in the story, rather than recognise this progress and encourage the new behaviours. In supervision, it emerged that the therapist tended, with her patient, to have the symbiotic relationship she herself had had with her parental figures, particularly her mother. As she was a therapist in clinical analysis, I decided to discuss the analysis of personal aspects in a different setting. Instead, we talked about her patient's need to be encouraged in that delicate period of change, and the fact that she, too, as a therapist needed encouragement. I therefore underlined that if the patient was facing social situations in a new way, this might be due to the good work they had been doing together, and that this recognition might be good for both of them, without analysing in depth all the details.

CHAPTER EIGHT

The phases of the therapeutic process

W hat happens in the therapist's room that can explain the changes we see between the beginning and the end? And most of all, what happens during the time of a psychotherapeutic process which usually goes from two to three years? And how can this path be explained by Transactional Analysis? From Berne to Erskine (1997) to Novellino (1998; 2004; 2012) and Moiso (Moiso & Novellino, 2000), there have been several classifications of strategic phases of therapy with TA. In the language I propose, I substantially follow the reference models and add a descriptive aspect of how psychotherapy develops in time. I particularly stress and underline the course of the analysis of the script, that is, a deep restructuring of one's personality through the description of what the therapist is doing at each phase. I also indicate when using the group as a tool can be appropriate to achieve the established goals. In fact, it can be helpful to end the phases of treatment in a group setting (in some cases from phase four, always from phase six).

1. First interviews
2. Contract and alliance
3. Returning control to the Adult

4. Restructuring the internal Parent
5. Listening to the Child and working on confusion liberating the Child from the demon and the Parent's blackmail
6. Consolidating boundaries accompanying the patient to choices free from the old script
7. Supporting the patient during separation, that is, leaving one's home with best wishes from one's parents.

Phase one: first interviews

What does the therapist do in the first interviews? First of all, she listens. Then, she gives information, explains the setting, proposes an administrative contract (payment, schedule, duration of sessions, rules about the relationship), and agrees with the person she is meeting to give feedback about the problems dealt with and an evaluation of the possibility of undergoing psychotherapy, or the necessity of having pharmacological treatment or other kinds of medical treatment and diagnostic checks. While these issues are dealt with in a conversation that involves the Adult psychological ego state of the client and the therapist, on an ulterior level the psychological exchange between the two people is deeper. In TA we say that the client's Child "smells" and looks for the therapist's Parent to see if he will be able to help the client. However, if the client is very confused and is used to choosing confirmations to his destructive script, he might search in the therapist for another "Joey"—as Berne said in *Games People Play* (1964)—or someone who will, anyway, confirm that changing or asking for help is useless. The ulterior level of the conversation may thus contain a beginning of dysfunctional games, and the confused Child is likely to try and hook ingenuous and distracted therapists. The archaic Parent of the client might even be looking for confirmation of the fact that no one can make you stop drinking or change your life. When you meet some particular patients, there seems to be someone inside them who is afraid of being killed by the therapist, and sometimes the disturbed Parent or the crazy Child shows how they are going to do everything it takes not to die, and might even hamper therapy and prevent change. In the first sessions, the two people who meet have a very intense transactional exchange, and most of what is going to happen later is already announced in a few cryptic lines, or in each other's way of introducing himself or herself. Only experience and a careful process of analysis of the first sessions will enable the therapist not to start the most dangerous games, or cross transactions too early in the process. In fact, if this happens, the client might not come back, and therapy would not begin.

Phase two: contract and alliance

In the first interviews, we agreed with the client about a psychotherapeutic path. From this moment on, since we have gone beyond the initial consulting and have turned the request for the first session into a "therapeutic contract", we can call him or her a patient. A therapeutic contract means defining a realistic objective we aim at attaining together through the tools provided by clinical dialogue. Sometimes the contract can be formulated in the first sessions, but it often requires longer elaboration. Formulating a contract is itself the result of an initial process of decontamination. In fact, the patient's initial requests (e.g., "I want to be able to leave my wife" or "I don't want to be anxious anymore") can sometimes be misleading, and they must be carefully analysed. The anxiety the patient feels might be a precise signal that he must change his lifestyle, and that very feeling of anxiety is perhaps the only healthy internal stimulus he is receiving; if it were deadened, his health might be in serious danger. As for his request for help to leave his wife, it must be said that at the beginning of a relationship the therapist usually knows little to evaluate whether this is a realistic and healthy objective. Only later on will it be possible to understand whether the problem is about separating or establishing a bond and being capable of intimacy. What actually differentiates a therapist from any other listener is the competence to place the requests within a system that decodes the whole functioning of the person, to analyse whether the request is congruous and whether it is possible to solve a symptom by conferring meaning on it. The specific skill is thus to help the patient choose a contract which is really helpful for him.

Making a good therapeutic contract thus implies having attained some basic goals: I know what my problem is, what I need in order to solve it, how much I am willing to invest in a psychotherapeutic path and in belief that the person I have chosen as a therapist can help me with this. A good contract is like an estimated budget or a work plan. If the preliminary analysis is well defined, this means that therapist and patient have already carried out part of the work, and are allied. By therapeutic alliance is meant that particular favourable relationship which is necessary in order to share one's deepest thoughts and feelings, work together on the analysis of the important choices in one's life, and agree about the pathway chosen in order to achieve the pre-established goals. Alliance is built slowly with those people who do not usually trust others and are used to relying only on themselves, and it is always the result of a decontamination process. Sometimes, patients who seem extremely trustful are only energised in their Adapted Child and may eventually disappear from the setting without even telling the therapist or ever having criticised a single thing. On the other hand, patients who are polemical and critical during the session, trust the therapist more than the ones who try to please her. The alliance is established, on the part of the therapist, on an emotional level when she is willing to be in a relationship with that specific person, to listen with sincere interest, and be committed both emotionally and professionally in therapy. A therapist who is emotionally distant from the patient might not create that friendly climate conducive to intimate conversation and exchange free from criticisms and prejudices. Patients sometimes say that there was something they did not feel free to tell the therapist and that they felt criticised, just as by a strict parent. This perception may be the result of a transference projection from the patient, but often it is neither analysed nor re-elaborated. By not doing this, the obstacle that was present in the previous significant relationships in the patient's life remains, and this new experience, too, confirms the patient's script and does not become an opportunity for restructuring and learning. A fair agreement between two Adults, empathy between Child and Child, and respect between the Parents, are the conditions conducive to trust and to the competence we define as a "therapeutic alliance".

Phase three: returning control to the Adult

In TA, this is the strategic phase of decontamination. The term is used according to the concept of structural contamination of ego states. If the Adult ego state is not mentally free from the confusion generated by the Child's phobias and the Parent's prejudices, the Adult's decisional power can be very limited. The therapeutic conversation, with explanations on the whiteboard about the thoughts the patient is describing, enables the Adult, who is observing and is allied with us during the conversation, to restrain the decisional power of archaic fears and judgments. The person can actually rapidly feel better if he cognitively understands what is being experienced. The rapid improvement TA often brings about is due to the fact that giving a simple and non-pathological name to one's suffering creates a sense of emotional reassurance. Sharing a language with the therapist to understand how a panic attack begins, or how a destructive conflict in the family came about, or how one can learn to control impulsiveness and anxiety, is extremely reassuring. In this period of therapy, the techniques of therapeutic operations of interrogation, specification, and confrontation are used together with explanations and illustrations with diagrams of ego states, transactions, and games. A TA therapist thus carries out cognitive work with her patients. However, this does not necessarily involve homework, unless there is a specific clinical necessity that, only for some patients, represents a way of exploring the functioning of the internal Child. Sharing the language on ego states, transactions, games, and script strengthens the alliance with the patient's Adult, the underpinning principle being that the Adult part must be activated if we want to work together with the patient on the change. At the meta-level of the effective relationship are two Adults who sit and talk, as they want to achieve the same goal, and two Parents who reach an agreement about the emotional climate that allows their child to enjoy his experiences and learning with curiosity and joyful interest.

Phase four: restructuring the internal Parent

The Parent introjected by those who experience strong anxiety or depression due to a sense of guilt is usually a rigid model, critical rather than protective. It is not conducive to healing—on the contrary, it paves the way for stress, which is self-produced, even independently from external stimuli. Differently, for others, what seems to be absent or malfunctioning is the internal Parent acting as a guide and protecting them from exposure to dangerous impulses and challenges, as if a child lived alone on the street trying to learn everything at his own expense. A therapist's job is to try to recognise how the model of the patient's internal Parent works, how it has been formed over the years, what its relationship with the historical parents and significant figures of the past is for the patient, in order to decide whether the inner guide is weak and therefore needs integrating. The introjected models are often past-oriented, they tend to function according to a world which no longer exists. Even if they did have some kind of internal coherence, this may no longer be appropriate or helpful to guide us into today and towards the future. A good introjected Parent, both in its normative and in its protective function, is a flexible guide that does not teach us our way according to an archaic route, but on the contrary acts as a compass when the GPS batteries are low. That is to say, it contains in itself the possibility to go beyond what is known and usual, and thus is the possibility to explore new worlds, to establish new rules. Nowadays, in a rapidly changing world, people decide to see a therapist even though they feel healthy, as they know they need to become more flexible and to continue their learning process as adults too. Indeed, when history goes at the fast pace that it currently does, lifelong rigid certainties cannot work, and a person who might have been healthy fifty years ago is likely to become ill today if he does not become stronger and learn to cope with change. One should undergo effective psychotherapy in order to survive in worlds like the one described in "Avatar", a wonderful post-modern fairy tale about the issues we are faced with. It is necessary to be connected in more complex neural networks than the ones our fathers had. This is why restructuring the internal Parent will always be part of in-depth psychotherapy, in which the therapist will have just a few years in which to play her hand—deep, powerful interventions and significant support. We will hardly ever have more than three years for therapeutic treatment, and often have a much shorter time.

Phase five: free the Child from confusion and destructive impulses

While therapist and patient proceed with the strategic phases described above, the Child's fear, his assumptions and survival decisions—sometimes dangerous and delirious—and impulsiveness of the internal "demon", as Berne called it, emerge. Information about how the historical child got hurt, what he did in order to receive attention and gratification, and how his parental figures were blackmailed and kept in check, must always be kept in mind during psychotherapy. In this sense, it is fundamental that a psychotherapist not be confused or contaminated, maybe by the idea that children are always good and that one can become a healthy adult just by removing too-strict rules or erasing the traces left by too-oppressive parents. Nobody would nowadays openly agree with such ingenuous eighteenth-century-like thoughts based on Rousseau's thinking, but I see that therapists often act as if they did agree with them. The Child ego state we deal with in psychotherapy is not only the Child oppressed with over-adaptation. It is often a Child who is blocked in his regressive archaic needs. Sadistic and perverse aspects, as well as impulsiveness, may emerge too, and may lead to fatal choices and titanic challenges which one should get rid of in order to live. We currently observe that there are several pathologies of the Child part of personality, among which we find borderline disorder and other personality disorders. This is why therapeutic treatments in therapeutic communities working with drug, alcohol, gambling, and sex addictions, are not effective enough to make deep change stable: in this kind of treatment, the work of deconfusion of the Child and of psychosomatic restructuring of his relationship with pleasure and control is not carried out. The same goes for various eating disorders, and, basically, for every disorder that is an expression of psychic pain or pleasure through the body. In redecisional TA, this work was carried out with regressive groups, with gestalt techniques, and by working on overcoming an impasse. In psychodynamic TA, it is done by using psychoanalytic interpretation and by working on dreams and transferences.

It is actually a complex and deep phase, involving the exploration of secret worlds, fantasies, dreams, and behavioural manifestations out of Parental control and Adult awareness, such as acting out and compulsions. And that is not all! Such in-depth work implies relearning the functioning of the Child ego state which is new as far as pleasure, most archaic needs, the relationship with one's body, and activating new neural circuits that trace new pathways, are concerned. This being the aim, psychodynamic TA groups are probably the most effective tool, as they give an opportunity to work on different levels and create the most appropriate context both for relearning and for choosing imitative—and therefore archaic—functioning strategies.

Phase six: reinforcing boundaries, experiencing new choices

In the last phases of psychotherapy, experiments and new behaviours are explored, and the patient accordingly expects from the therapist, and the group, acknowledgment and applause which act as helpful reinforcement. When a person is deeply changing, his script is usually not supported by what is familiar and by the social environment that he has lived in until this moment. It is as if no one recognises you; and groups, as everyone knows, tend to be conformist and expect every member to respond to the expectations the group has about the role each has been assigned. If a person usually pays for everyone's breakfast, if friends are used to going to his house, and he is popular because he is generous (which sometimes leads to exploitation), this person may lose popularity and appreciation when he tries to escape from this role. This is what gives rise to the prejudice according to which people who undergo psychotherapy become more "selfish" and "self-centered". In fact, if psychotherapy has been effective, social and affective relationships will be affected by it, and become deeper and more sincere, but less adapted to conformist models and habitual roles. The patient might thus go through a rough period, in which friends and relatives might openly say: "Stop, because it's doing you no good", "I no longer recognise you", and he might end up alone. In this delicate period of experimentation of new social behaviours, the therapist must necessarily be supportive, as the patient might oscillate between new and old, or fear being isolated and lose acknowledgment from others. Going on means finding advantages and discovering sincere affectionate people who do not try to exploit you. A person who has always played for affection by doing a lot for others, for example, can feel a strong sense of anxiety when he starts to say "no".

Phase seven: separating, leaving home full of energy

When changes are somewhat consolidated, and the therapist is not worried about a possible destructive regression, the moment to separate arrives. The end of therapy is both a graduation party and a tearful goodbye at the station. It is a patient's right to be a bit scared and anxious, just like any son or daughter who leaves the parents' house for good. On the other hand, just like a balanced parent, the therapist must determinedly and firmly support the patient and encourage him to take this step. Nowadays, we may find patients who would be in endless therapy, especially if the therapy fee were easily affordable, as if it were a weekly massage in a well-being centre. However, if we consider psychotherapy as a cure, it must have an end, and actually the ending itself is a learning phase. One learns to properly say goodbye, to autonomously carry out self-analysis, and to experience an ending that does not imply tragedies, abandonment, and dramas. For the end of therapy in TA we usually talk about a final contract or a contract about closure, which is agreed upon several months before the actual conclusion, which then happens in three sessions or groups. It can be the patient who suggests conclusion, or the therapist can suggest that the patient think about it. As a matter of fact, discussing this issue usually gives rise to a rich and fruitful exchange. It is the time in which illuminating dreams emerge, fantasies which help in supporting the psychic elaboration of separation. In psychoanalytic terms, we might say this is the phase of mourning elaboration, almost to underline the experience of change which is taking place, as if it basically represents a loss. It is actually a time characterised by sadness because we will not see each other again, but also by joy at the success, or the pleasure of keeping inside oneself the image of the therapist introjected as a protective internal presence, usually a much better figure than the real person we are leaving. This protective, reassuring, blessing presence, as well as a voice that challenges us and confronts us with truth about ourselves, will not be abandoned: we will carry it with us.

That's enough. The real person, in this period, may even disappoint us or make us angry, or sometimes be boring. It is the right time to part, better if we shake hands and thank each other. I often hear myself tell therapists: "We must leave the stage when it's time." If we can separate and we know the immense resource the possibility of saying goodbye and leaving contains, then, and only then, can we teach it to others. To anyone who is ending a psychotherapy path I can say that you learn a lot from moments like these, just as in ordinary life we sometimes tell all we have to tell only at the end: indeed, the intensity of emotional exchanges or messages of a definitive goodbye give us an opportunity to acquire awareness of the richness we have inside us and of the relevance of this important human experience.

CHAPTER NINE

Script therapy

What is the script?

Am I a human being free to decide my destiny or is my path heavily determined from the outside? Is my life an original story or does it repeat patterns and choices others have made in my place?

Such questions are indeed inevitable when, with the inexorable passing of time, we stop to think near a river. We may ask questions that are simpler, but just as relevant: Was it really me who wanted to have children? Did I really intend to take over the family firm, or be a doctor, or quit studying and start working so early? People usually ask themselves these questions when some external event acts as a stimulus and provokes them, as if their personal certainties were safely closed in a fortress that is being besieged.

I remember a young woman who got married when she was about twenty. She worked as a clerk, had a beautiful house, her life seemed to be well-balanced and harmonious, she had lots of friends, belonged to a religious community, and was considered a good family girl.

The destabilising event in her life happened all of a sudden: a dear friend of hers confesses to her that she has fallen in love with another woman and feels she is a lesbian; at the same time, one of her female colleagues falls in love with her and tells her about it. The woman's first reaction is to be outraged, and she invites her friend to repent, as she considers what is happening to her friend to be a symptom of mental confusion. However, a few months later she herself has a lesbian relationship with a colleague of hers, starts psychotherapy, and leaves her husband. The work of analysis the woman starts at this point in her story, implies that she has decided to confront herself with several issues that can no longer be denied. The emotional storm, the tragedy she has been living through, will not let her sweep things under the carpet, as has happened with other stories. This young woman is in search of the truth about herself, since what she feels does not allow her to live two parallel lives, although this might have been easier for her social environment. In different, less dramatic situations, questions about one's life are asked when one is in one's forties, when perhaps the objective established by the family script has been attained and one feels at peace with the duties of the parental programme.

An example of another young woman: "I graduated in chemistry, I work in industry, I earn a lot of money, I have proven to you that I can make it, so now I can finally leave everything and have a new start" she will tell her parents.

Over the years, I have often seen people who, at some time in their lives, decided to call into question all their assumptions. Some of them dreamed of a life that they considered impossible to achieve, and they tried to experience something similar by having secret affairs far from their families, gambling, or traveling to exotic places, so as to experience moments of pause and the perception of different identities. I have also seen people who decided to take dance lessons in their forties or fifties, learn to sail or go photography trekking. They were creating new opportunities for hobbies, work, and adventure that gradually became their new identity. Thus, the clerk defined himself as a tango dancer, and if he was good and lucky enough, he could even become a famous dancer or dance teacher; and again, the technician who worked in a private firm could become a free sailor who sailed the sea on his own, or an adventurous explorer.

When I hear such stories, I always reflect about coercion—the compulsion to repeat—and freedom. I see that some people are happy in their autonomy while others are happy with their bonds and their apparent submission to others, some are subdued, and some are struggling. Of course, not everyone looks for freedom. For many, the main search in life is for a sense of belonging and certainties, which strongly contrast with independence and self-determination. The script is the mental scheme that every human being has already created in his childhood according to parental influences, genetic conditioning, and first relational experiences. This scheme determines the subsequent interpretations of events, the choices associated with these interpretations, and the related feelings, as in writing a theatre script of a role in a comedy, a tragedy, or a glorious, heroic story of success.

Berne wrote that the concept of script has its roots in Freud's theories. However, differently from what happened in a psychoanalytic approach, the script is a drama which is really acted out in society, and not only in a patient's head. Berne compares his concept of script with Jung's concept of archetypes as models that influence individual choices, with the concept of the Oedipus complex, and Adler's idea of life plan. Differently from Adler, Berne claims that the life plan is not completely unconscious and does not depend only on the individual, but, on the contrary, is deeply influenced by the environment and parental relationship. Berne said that

> The forces of human destiny are foursome and fearsome: demonic parental programming, abetted by the inner voice the ancients called the Daemon; constructive parental programming, aided by the thrust of life called Physis long ago; external forces, still called Fate; and independent aspirations, for which the ancients had no human name, since for them such were the privileges mainly of gods and kings. (Berne, 1972, p. 56)

And again, Berne writes:

> The script scene began long ages past, when life first oozed out of the mud and began to transmit the results of its experiences chemically, through genes [...]. This chemical branch culminated in the spider, who spins his strange circular geometry without instruction. In his case, the script is written in fixed molecules of organic acids (DNA) [...]. In man, too, the genes determine chemically some of the patterns he must follow, and from which he cannot deviate [...] Many a man with the chemistry of a great ballet dancer spends his time dancing with other people's dishes in a lunchroom, and others with the genes of a mathematician pass their days juggling

other people's papers in the back room of a bank or bookie joint. But within his chemical limitations, whatever they are, each man has enormous possibilities for determining his own fate. (Berne, 1972, p. 63)

Existential positions

Berne states that in the first year of life we select a basic emotional position about existence according to a primitive, pre-logic intuitive opinion about life, ourselves, and what we can expect from others:

+ + constructive position, I'm OK, you're OK
– + depressive position, I'm not OK, you're OK
+ – projective position, I'm OK, you're not OK
– – futility position, I'm not OK, you're not OK

Every person in life tends to have a preconceived attitude about the events and, in particular, ambiguous episodes that can be interpreted in different ways. The initial existential position can explain why the same event can even be experienced and interpreted in contradictory ways.

Protocol within the first two years

The events that constitute the protocol, the first foundation of the psychological script, happen in very early childhood, according to Berne within the first two years of life, and are determined by the interactions with the figures nowadays defined as attachment figures. Berne's theory of protocol is indeed connected with the most recent theories about attachment, which have confirmed through scientific observation the existence of different types of primary relationships which affect the rest of one's entire affective life.

The script apparatus

The need to structure and simplify the way the script is structured in a child's mind leads Berne to explain which processes and messages are defined within the first six years of life, and this is what he calls script apparatus, made up of:

Script curse or payoff: a command such as "Disappear" or "Drop dead!" (death sentences) or "Become rich and famous for me", "Follow in my footsteps" (life sentences): the parents tell a child how he has to end his life.

Injunctions or stoppers: parents give an unfair negative command perhaps given by a crazy Child ego state or a sadistic Critical Parent which actually does not let the child ignore the command associated with the payoff, for example, "Don't succeed!" or "Don't be more important than me because I could destroy you" or even just "Don't be yourself, be what I expect you to be."

Provocations: challenges from parent to child in order to encourage him towards the script payoff. Such messages often come from a demon, a crazy Child ego state in the parent. An example can be "Try and drink more than me."

Counter-script slogan: how to spend time waiting for the action, for the drama. These messages come from the Nurturing Parent, for example "Work hard" or "Save as much money as you can" (perhaps to then waste everything by gambling).

Programme: what the child must know about real life, how things are to be done, how it is appropriate to behave socially.

Child's or demon's impulses: the needs and impulses that fight against the script apparatus.

Exorcism: inner liberation from the curse. Some scripts have a hidden built-in element, for example, "If you go through this ordeal—like the twelve labours of Hercules—you will be free."

"This is the anatomy of the script apparatus: curse, injunction and provocation are the script controls, while the other four items can be used to fight them", Berne writes.

I currently think that the demon in the child often represents a dangerous force, if the Parent that has been internally structured is not a good Wizard who can keep the Child's impulses under control. I say this because I have been working for a long time with borderline cases, especially drug-addicts with severe difficulties in controlling their impulses, and according to my experience, healing cannot be attained unless a patient with these kinds of problems restructures a powerful Normative and Nurturing Parent who can keep impulses under control. In fact, in such cases, healing implies permanently giving up behaviours of use and abuse of substances, or other addictions. For some patients, the fight against the inner demon lasts all their lives.

The Child impulse in Letizia:
the possessed woman

I have known Letizia since she was twenty-six and was in a therapeutic community for drug-addicts. The community director called me because Letizia had been causing trouble, she rebelled against rules, she tried to escape and took others with her. In addition, over the previous few months, she had been suffering from terrible "pseudo convulsive" crises which she defined as "possessed-like" and which had scared the whole community and made everyone want to throw her out. When I was called over, the social worker who personally followed Letizia wasn't working because of depression and stress; the woman was convinced that her illness was due to Letizia's negative force. The director asked me to follow Letizia as a therapist, after her expulsion from the community. I accepted only on condition that she could stay within the community and that she was willing to undergo psychological treatment. In the first interviews, Letizia told me her story. She came from a disintegrated Slavic family; her mother was a prostitute, her father was an alcoholic, and she was the youngest of four sisters. She remembered she had been sent to an institution when she was five, after being sexually abused by her mother's lover. When she was nine, she was adopted, together with her sister, who was two years older; the two elder sisters had previously been taken away from the family, and Letizia did not know anything about one of them. She said that her adoptive mother was a crazy woman full of superstitions, who practiced magic rituals and spells, and her adoptive father was a subdued man. Letizia said that her adoptive mother had cast a spell on her and that she was possessed and that everyone who took care of her would fall sick just as her social worker had done. She told me she was very worried about me, as her mother was evil and very powerful. I replied that my magic was powerful too, and that I was not scared, although I could see that very negative forces were involved.

Letizia was really sick, she had been drinking and using drugs since she was fifteen, had a serious eating disorder, ate very little and only some kinds of food, and she often threw up after meals. About her crises, which only started some months after she had joined the therapeutic community, she said she was possessed by the devil. I asked the director to call me immediately if she had had a "crisis", so I personally saw these terrible scenes in which Letizia, frothing at the mouth and vomiting a green liquid, threw herself on to the windowsill to jump off, and destroyed everything she could find; four men had to hold her for about half an hour to calm her down. After the crisis, she seemed exhausted and she did not remember anything about it. I discussed with her the possibility of her being hospitalised in the psychiatry department should a similar episode occurr again, because she was too dangerous, both to herself and to others, in that situation. So, when her second crisis occurred, I called an ambulance and organised her hospitalisation. The doctors in the department of psychiatry discussed this case for a long time, and she was hospitalised three times that month, until I finally found out that she caused these violent organic pains herself by drinking some methylated spirit she had stolen from the cleaning room. This explained the frothing at the mouth and the symptoms of poisoning that accompanied the dissociative crisis. Here was the demon in action: once the phenomenon was discovered and analysed, Letizia started behaving more appropriately.

Giulia's demon: the viper's poisoned kiss

Giulia is a twenty-eight-year-old woman, an engineer working, with great enthusiasm, in a telecommunications firm. She begins psychotherapy because she has been strongly urged to do so by her fiancé, who tells her: "I think you have some problems, and if you don't seek therapy I will leave you because you are too dangerous and you hurt everyone who loves you." Giulia tells me that her mother died when she was fifteen, she has got a brother who is two years younger, and her relationship with her father is quite cold; according to what she says, he has never really shown a deep interest in his children. She tells me she comes from a city in the south and that she has been away from home for several years because she attended university in a city in the north and did not go back to her town of origin. Giulia has begun seeing a psychotherapist because she has slept with nearly all the male friends in her group and many colleagues at work. She says that she often finds herself in absurd situations in which she sleeps with a man, then feels guilty and confesses to the wife/fiancée/companion of her occasional lover, and to her boyfriend too. In particular, she has recently been involved in an intrigue, because she had sex with a dear friend of hers who was going to get married, and she decided to tell everyone about "the betrayal", including their fiancé(e)s, imagining that the wedding would be cancelled. However, her friend had "forgiven" them and said that what happened did not really change things, and everything would go back to normal. At that point Giulia entered an apparently depressive state, and her fiancé told her: "You are not normal, I will leave you if you don't seek therapy", and he sent her to a therapist.

Giulia's child demon compelled her to constantly seduce and manipulate others, and she particularly felt an irresistible impulse to sleep with other women's men, even by getting them drunk or pretending there was a very strong intellectual connection between her and them, which of course disappeared when the game ended with the confession to the other woman. Giulia was not aware she was so angry, like a child who bites everyone around her, nor did she realise that this situation would lead to her being left alone, without the intimacy she seemed to desire and that she challenged when she found it in other couples. Her relational attitude was typically borderline, hers was a loveless script. In fact, after a few months of therapy, she began playing the same games with her new boss at work, and her fiancé left her and told her: "I'm leaving you to your therapist, you are too poisonous, I no longer want to deal with you." End of game. A few months later, Giulia quits psychotherapy when she gets a colleague of hers to marry her. She will leave him shortly afterwards, despite therapeutic indications not to take significant sentimental decisions in that period.

The demon inside Giovanni: Doctor Jekyll and Mr. Hyde

Giovanni is an entrepreneur, he's forty years old, and the director of an insurance agency. He is brilliant, good-looking, has a lot of responsibilities, is married to a beautiful, rich young woman, and has two eight-month-old twin girls. He starts therapy because his wife and his young lover have asked him to. They agreed to have him follow a psychological treatment as he had threatened to commit suicide if one of them decided to leave him. Giovanni tells me he has always been correct both at work and in his interpersonal relationships. However, he has felt confused for the past year and a half because he has fallen in love with a young woman who works in the office, and he can no longer live his life. He says he cannot stand being far from this woman, he feels desperate if she tries to leave him, and if she does not answer his phone calls, he thinks of suicide. His wife is a great friend, a wonderful woman who was in his class at high school. He declares he no longer loves her, and yet he cannot leave her. He never mentions his two daughters in this conflict, but he answers my questions saying that his daughters were born through artificial insemination, which he had consented to only for his wife, while he was actually already in love with the other woman. This disastrous situation was brought to light because he had told his lover that he was about to separate from his wife, and at the same time he told his wife that everything was OK. The two women eventually met and told each other their versions of the story. He started threatening both of them, saying that he would kill himself, as his lover tried to leave him and both Giovanni's and his wife's families of origin are involved in this intricate matter, with inevitable disastrous interventions. His mother criticises him, tries to speak to the young woman to convince her to go away so as not to destroy Giovanni's family, and so on.

When I meet Giovanni for the first time, he is extremely confused. He tells everyone that he is really depressed, so that people will not judge him or ask him to take responsibility for this disaster. As a matter of fact, in the interviews, Giovanni admits this is not the first time he has been involved in intrigues, lies, and mess. It has happened at least once before. When he was twenty-eight, he organised his graduation party, but he had not actually taken exams for years, although he had convinced his parents that he was going to graduate. Until that moment, he had been a perfect son. When a friend of Giovanni's went to talk to his parents before the party and told them the truth, Giovanni managed to cope with disappointment and surprise only by entering depression. After a one-year-crisis, he was forgiven, and he started working in the insurance agency he would take over a few years later. The "perfect boy" thus tended to have a double life every time he had to face a choice which might disappoint someone. His compromise with rules, with his internal and external Parent, was to pretend, so that he did not have to confront anyone and, like Jekyll and Hyde, tried to separate two lives and hide them even to himself, if only he could. When he was unmasked, he said he felt bad, that he thought he would die, and he had even told his family—even his parents-in-law and his lover—that he had suddenly remembered being abused by a neighbour when he was ten, and that the memory of this trauma haunted him all the time. In this project, the role of therapy was for him to say: "You see, as long as I'm feeling so bad and seeing a therapist, you can't ask anything of me, I can't leave my lover, decide about my marriage or even take care of my daughters because I'm so insane I can't be responsible!" Giovanni's family of origin was simple, strict, and conformist. He had a dependent and conflictual relationship with his mother who always criticised him, and with whom he avoided confrontation by telling lies. He took an almost perverted pleasure in looking for support from women and inventing stories in which it was always the other's fault.

Mina and Gianni: how to punish your parents if they are strict

Mina's inner demon had her exacerbate her mother's disorder; the woman had always been obsessed by cleaning and by controlling passion, food, or sex in the same way. Similarly Mina, when she starts suffering from a serious obsessive-compulsive disorder, continuously washes her hands until they are extremely frail and transparent, until the skin comes off. She also started obsessively washing every piece of clothing that has any kind of contact with the environment outside her family house—the trousers that touch the chair at work, the coat someone had involuntarily touched while she was walking in the street, and so on—until she almost drove her mother, with whom she lived, crazy. For the therapist who is listening, the wicked game between Mina and her mother is quite relevant in order to understand and solve the symptom. The two women are challenging each other, and at the same time Mina's demon child is punishing Mina's mother: I'll show you how bad I can be thanks to what you've taught me. Just like King Midas, who was punished for his impulses, Mina punishes herself and her mother through behaviour that becomes paradoxical, since she has strictly followed the rigid parental rules and made them even more extreme.

In the same way, Gianni, who is twenty-three years old, and suffers from a very serious obsessive-compulsive disorder, punishes his two parents, who have to take care of him in everything he does, through a disorder of "a labyrinth of words". He cannot do anything unless he follows in his mind a connection of words associated one with another, and unless he remembers the exact sequence of words his brain will not give the impulse to eat, walk, speak, and communicate, and so on. His parents are two old intellectual people who raised their son as a little genius, over-stimulating his linguistic curiosity and neglecting his affective needs or intimate contact. Gianni begins to suffer from this disorder during his adolescence, and wraps his parents up in a spider-web made of words and paralysis, from which they cannot escape. As they go to several psychiatric hospitals and speak to numerous important doctors, Gianni becomes confused too, and is trapped in his own labyrinth.

The demon in general

In therapy I have often observed destructive behaviours that start from the Child ego state, sometimes evidently over-adapted and sometimes rebellious, and at other times impulsive behaviours that were surprising because of how disconnected from thought (Adult) and protection (internal Parent) they were. Such destructive behaviours are more evident in personalities with bipolar disorder, but they can be found in borderline cases as well. Sometimes I have observed these same impulses to hurt oneself and others in people with serious obsessive-compulsive disorders.

How do we intervene on the demon in psychotherapy?

It is very likely that, as we approach the deepest phases of the therapeutic work, we are bitten and attacked by the demon. It is fine if, in psychotherapy, the demon manifests itself by attacking the therapist's Parent, with criticisms and acting-outs, because as long as they happen in a protected setting, the therapist can analyse and deal with such tests. It is as if the child were screaming: "Are you strong enough to let me come even if I'm so bad? Are you good enough not to die of my poison? Are you powerful and kind enough not to destroy me with your anger?" The demon can manifest itself with small or great attacks on the setting: the patient forgets to come, does not pay, accuses the therapist of things that are not true. An expert therapist knows that the demon is just a frightened child that bites. However, he or she does not underestimate how dangerous impulses are, as they may even lead a person to suicide, madness, or murder with really tragical script endings. Especially if we are seeing people with tragic scripts, this is the moment for the highest protection. In these moments, it can be useful to phone a patient who has not attended for a while, invite him for an interview if he has stopped coming, sometimes setting up non-suicide or protection contracts. In the case of patients with serious addictions or bipolar disorders, I always set up a contract in which the patient authorises me to inform a doctor or someone from the family about a risk of suicide or if the patient shows the deliberate intention to hurt himself by suddenly interrupting the psychopharmacological therapy without the therapist's consent. I have used such protective methods in two cases over the last two years, and each time I had been authorised by the patients: one was a woman with two little children who risked hurting them physically because from time to time she stopped taking antipsychotic drugs (I was the only one to notice, so I called her husband and he agreed with her psychiatrist to send her to hospital, thus protecting their children). The other case was when I called the brothers of a patient who threatened to commit suicide, and informed the doctor and the local psychiatric service about what was going on.

In TA psychotherapy, such moments are moments of deconfusion, of deep and interpretative work on the Child ego state, which often causes the disorder, as a solution and compromise with the crazy Parent. It is a delicate period of the psychotherapeutic work, in which the therapist must constantly focus on risky behaviours (including the danger due to driving too fast or drinking too much), and protection must be active in contractual accordance with the internal Parent and with understanding on the part of the patient's Adult. The therapist acts as a parental model: "I accept you the way you are, even when you are desperate, and I won't let you hurt yourself; I will teach you how you can face such intense feelings and terrible fears without hurting yourself."

Script therapy is in-depth psychotherapy, it requires years of work because it supports a person in the restructuring of his inner world of beliefs, basic emotions, attitudes, and behaviours, which steadily change, because in the therapeutic relationship there is the highly relevant reparative element of an attachment relationship. It is as if the patient has to understand, find his origins, rediscover his primary needs, and internalise a new and more effective Parent that manifests itself through healthier protection and rules to be followed, according to the Child's impulses and needs.

CHAPTER TEN

Group therapy

A psychotherapy group that follows Berne's Transactional Analysis model is a treatment in which the therapist has weekly meetings with a group of adults whose aim is to handle some changes, solve a symptom, or even just analyse their script through psychotherapy. The group is thus like a metaphorical container in which psychotherapy takes place; the participants are committed to maintaining confidentiality and must be ready to give and receive feedback on what is said and what happens in the group. One usually enters a group after a period of individual therapy, either short or long—one month to a year—and each member will work to attain his contract goal by using the group relationships to test the change he wants to achieve, as in a laboratory. For example, a person can enter a group to solve a pathological shyness that makes him withdraw from many social situations and feel strongly distressed at parties or during coffee-breaks at work. This person will enter the group thinking that the same distress that makes him withdraw is going to occur in this context too. Indeed, this will really happen in the therapy group. However, this behaviour will be noticed and analysed. Then, we will inquire into the fears that are activated by the interpersonal group relationships, until the patient is able to identify different ways to establish a contact and relearn more satisfactory behaviours that the group will constructively reinforce. Such a shy person usually has a very strict and persecutory internal Parent who acts like an eye watching from above and causes him to feel embarrassed, as if he were naked, dirty, or inadequate, whatever he says or does. This person, accordingly, will be awkward and sometimes ridiculous until he obtains confirmation of his worst fears.

When a person enters a psychotherapy group, the intensity of the treatment is doubled, and the effects of the analytic process of change are heightened. In fact, dual therapy weaves together the analysis of one's past history and the exploration of a corrective and reparative relationship as far as transference is concerned. In the group, this is more thickly interwoven: the way in which I establish contact with the group members will describe myself as an individual, and the therapist will see my script enacted. The therapist obtains precious information that will help her make a more precise diagnosis and understand the problem. In addition, the therapist will have a chance to use transactions, strokes, and every interpersonal exchange, as in a laboratory where the inter-subjective psychic world and inter-subjective transactional world are repaired, corrected, and restructured.

We can see what happens in the attachment relationship enacted and expressed in the relationship with the therapist—as well as with brothers or sisters, males and females, sons and daughters. While one person tells his story aloud before an audience and interacts with these people in the microcosm of the group, an attachment relationship—with its dramas and ambivalences—is being relived and actualised, and we can see it enacted in everyone's transference dynamics. Daniel Stern would use the expression "*kairos* moment" to describe the group. *Kairos* is the present time, the favourable moment, the instant in which it is possible to change the course of destiny or the path of a star. In Greek culture, it is the moment at which something comes into being.

In the therapeutic relationship, not only is an old drama re-actualised, but a new experience arises. As this experience is brought into the light of consciousness, that is, it reaches emotional awareness and is told and shared, the suitable environment for a re-enactment—maybe even a restructuring of the script—is created. In the patients' minds, we therapists somehow become new parents. The group, too, becomes a new family and social container, in which the current relationship creates a proper space for a new path towards a sense of belonging that can be introjected more consciously and freely than the ones introjected in one's real historical childhood. Shifting from individual setting to group setting is particularly important for those who are stuck and cannot help looking back or keep reproducing, with the therapist, the drama of their primary dramatic experience. "I want you to be the mother I wanted and didn't have when I was four or six. I want you to be the father who didn't choose me as his princess" some people seem to be saying. "I don't want new things, I want to go back to that battle, then, and win this time, fill the void that there was at that time."

Entering a group means modifying the scene, introducing new stimuli, new actors, new themes. There are more chances to re-elaborate and solve the regressive aspects that the dual relationship sometimes may maintain and support. The group is a shock, it means being thrown into the world, or school, or children's games, or adolescents' games, or sexual dynamics connected with one's growth. "I am no longer the only one, I'm not your only focus, I'm not so special for you." It represents loss, and the child drastically lowers his expectations and fantasies. But at the same time: "I am no longer alone when you're not there, I'm with people of my own kind, I can look at myself in the mirror, play, spend my time, learn."

As we grow up, our mind grows in a network of interactions and social stimuli, and therefore our experiences enable us to increase the neural connections and, accordingly, the opportunities to find our way in the world and enjoy it. We currently know that our mind is intersubjective and that we constantly need to balance our being individuals separated from others at the same time as being part of a human community. This is the intersubjective motivational system that regulates the psychological dichotomy between belonging and isolation. The poles of this spectrum are, on the one hand, cosmic loneliness and, on the other, the mental phenomena of transparency, fusion, and disappearance of the self, as Stern declares. The exact point for well-being is different for each of us, and it depends on our role in the group, the other people there, and the history of our own relationships up to that moment. The position in this continuum is to be decided over and over again, and it is subjected to continuous corrections and adjustments. The discovery of mirror neurons proved the existence of the mental relationship we have with others: we participate in the others' actions as if we were doing that same action without having to imitate it. Our neurons "light up" when another person performs an action or expresses an emotion, thus making us able to feel the other, understand his action, and reproduce it. Resonance phenomenon is the capacity to bring about an emotional contagion, the capacity that makes possible empathy, sympathy, identification, and intersubjectivity. Adaptive oscillators are those neurobiological mechanisms that enable us to regulate and synchronise with others: the *pas de deux* and group dance are simple examples of this. People with empathic difficulties, difficulties in synchronising themselves with others—even just in their movements, or when they dance—probably need group therapy as a restructuring and learning experience, since the coping processes (the whole of cognitive and behavioural efforts to manage specific internal and/or external demands that are appraised as exceeding the person's resources, cf. Lazarus, 1991) probably did not work out well in that person's development.

Group therapy is indeed also a kind of retraining to tune in to others, to listen, to speak respecting one's turn, to recognise one's own and others' emotions in response to a stimulus, to exchange ideas and be competitive, to co-operate and build something together. According to this description, the group seems to be the summary of a healthy educational process, and in part it is. However, it is most of all a restructuring experience, because the adults before the therapist have by now acquired rigidly repetitive patterns of behaviour. In order to reactivate learning it is therefore necessary to analyse the processes that have led to certain rigid and pathological balances and to intervene "surgically" to remove some dysfunctional defences. The group setting recreates primary scenes, of when a person joined a group for the first time in the family or a social nucleus. Whoever enters a group is immersed in ancient emotions; everyone of us has sometimes felt like a child again, shy and embarrassed but also excited and curious, ready to perform a show or hide behind a curtain to take a peek at the people in the room and then run away. Group therapy thus gives us a chance to re-enact the script in its protocol and to become aware of its mechanisms. It gives us a chance to live a corrective and redecisional experience as far as attachment patterns are concerned. Most of all, it helps the person reinforce and energise the experience of the present (*kairos*), that is, learning— through resonance with others and awareness—to try out new solutions to old problems, learning from the here and now of relationships and group context. So, we can say that the group can be conducive to several important skills:

Tuning in to others, becoming able to feel empathy and sympathy.

Co-ordinate with others: for example, Aldo, who walked into doors and could not dance, Elisa, who spoke while others were speaking, without even looking at them.

Limiting resonance to others, if I am a person who risks fusion or symbiosis.

Listening to what others tell me so as to control my own behaviours.

Using the creative energy that only social exchange can provide.

Learning humour and intimacy in emotional exchange and in conversation.

Attaining change thanks to the group

The experience of group treatment offers a chance to relive the building of one's personal identity through mirroring in attachment relationships and in peer relationships.

In the time spent together in the group, thanks to the stimuli from the therapist and the setting, the group represents a chance to walk along an emotional and cognitive path that is unique and powerful:

to relive, in a brief period of time, the history of how one's script has been structured;

to observe how survival decisions have been taken;

to understand how decisions can be changed so as to have a wider range of options and therefore a chance to be well;

to give up unrealistic objectives that are unattainable;

to experience that in the world there is space for oneself and for the other person, for every human being;

to learn how to achieve pre-established goals, in a constructive way both for oneself and for others.

The treatment method basically considers that the therapist observes how each member introduces himself to the "micro-world" that is the group, and helps the patient develop a group imago, the mental image one has about oneself in the group and the group in relation to oneself.

In the concept of imago and its use in Berne's type of group lies the essential tool of a Transactional Analysis therapist.

Group imago is a concept illustrated by Berne when he describes the dynamics of groups and organisations as the mental picture of what the group is like that every person creates for himself when entering the group, and that contains fantasies and projections on to the group, the leader, and its members, projections due to past experiences, particularly to the primary group he belonged to (Berne, 1963).

That is to say, if I was welcomed when I was born because my parents had been waiting for me for a long time and really wanted to have me, and I was accepted into my parents' and my family's lives, I will probably expect from the new groups I will enter—at school, then at work or with friends—to be treated like that, and I will therefore be willing to enter new groups and perhaps be curious about new opportunities. The group imago might, in this case, contain the image of a warm, friendly place, where I have my own space, where I can find smiles, interesting stimuli, people who encourage and support me, as if I were already programmed to repeat experiences of exchange, conversation, and intimacy. A person with such characteristics is glad to enter a group, even a therapy group, although he probably does not really need to do it from a clinical point of view, since his experiences as a child have already created the emotional and cognitive condition and the behavioural maps for him to benefit as much as possible from being with other people. This person may ask to enter a group at a particular moment of his existence, perhaps to deal with a separation, process a mourning, or face a change. This is the kind of person we may meet on a training course, in counselling, or at the lessons of a master's degree, and the request that can be made to a psychotherapist is to be supported as a specific step in one's own growth. This person is very likely to be satisfied with psychotherapy, and our work as therapists with him will be completely successful, although we cannot really take credit for that. A person with a good coping strategy is able to learn from life and new experiences, if only he is stimulated. If a student loves learning, the teacher can even be just "OK". So, an "OK" honest therapist is good enough to cure a patient who has inside him the capacity to cure himself and to seize all the opportunities life offers him. On the other hand, it will take a really good teacher to motivate a student with difficulties. In this case, there must be a good teacher and a good therapist. Going back to the group and the concept of imago, the therapy group is like medicine or a treatment course for those patients who do not want to come to terms with difficulties or to enter the group.

A person who does not want to enter a group usually has a negative imago, and expects he will not be accepted or will have to fight to have his space, is embarrassed, is afraid he will not feel comfortable or be understood, thinks "I am so different from the rest of the world that the group won't be good for me."

If I am a person whose birth was not so easy, for example, I was born as an unexpected child or after an unsuccessful abortion, or when my mother or some other member of my family was sick, I will probably intuitively feel that there is not enough room for me in the world. If, then, I am the third or fourth child, I may be afraid I will have to fight to have a seat, to speak or to be listened to, to be seen by my parents, and I may similarly perceive the group as too tiring. There are some people, however, who, being the first-born, have had to substitute their parents and take care of the youngest children. They may re-propose this script in their lives as group leaders in society, like a team leader at work; if asked to enter a group, they may say: "It's difficult for me to be in a group if I'm not the leader." So, people who have the illusion of also being an only child in the world, where there are actually several billion of us, cannot even conceive of the group, even as a place to recruit followers. A therapeutic goal will thus be that such a person agrees to enter a group and, most important of all, stays after the first narcissistic wounds or disappointments. To have a patient imagine entering a therapy group is a very helpful exercise to enhance the diagnostic process. You learn a lot about a patient when group therapy is proposed and when you have a chance to observe him interacting with others.

Help patients to enable their group imago to evolve

The therapist's task is to recognise and analyse the level of the imago of each member of the group, and, most important of all, to support each participant in having his personal imago evolve to more mature levels of development and interaction with others. The group is a perfect place for a work of deconfusion and redecision regarding deep script issues. This is also the most complex skill to acquire as a group therapist: to be able to use every event of the group as a tool to be linked with the individual contract and redecisional development that the person needs requires great competence and a lot of concentration. The question a therapist is constantly thinking of is: how can each group member use this stimulus?

Before beginning

A person is the first to arrive at the evening meeting, and there is no one else in the room yet. The therapeutic question is: how do you feel about this event, and how is this related to your personal history and your script? Even if an event is fortuitous and is not determined by your actions, the way you describe the event to yourself is indeed connected to your script, the way you interpret and decode the events.

The examples I am about to give correspond to the four basic existential positions that in TA are described as pre-logical, emotional positions that every person activates in every circumstance as a filter of interpretation of events, of his own and the other's position in the event itself.

We define the constructive position as the "I'm OK, you're OK" attitude, usually described by the + + scheme. This means having an assertive attitude in every situation and decoding ambiguous events as events to be understood, not necessarily threatening. We define the depressive position as the "I'm not OK, you're OK" attitude, usually described by the – + scheme. A person in a depressive position tends to feel responsible in every difficult situation with others, whom he tends to justify and absolve, while confirming the sense of guilt for himself—and guilt will be the most recurring feeling.

We define the paranoid or projective position as the "I'm OK, you're not OK" attitude, usually described by the + – scheme. Those who are in a projective position always blame others and constantly defend themselves by being aggressive to the person who is talking to them, so as not to run the risk of being criticised or being seen making a mistake, which he cannot stand.

We define the futility position as the "I'm not OK, you're not OK" attitude, usually described by the – – scheme. This is the desperate and passive position of someone who gives up any chance to improve his own life, has a negative vision of himself and life, and does not trust anybody. Thus, in the scenario of setting a group meeting, a group member enters the room on time and finds no one there. What he will think, what emotions he will feel, and how he will behave, both in this circumstance and later, surely depends on the four different existential positions that act as a filter to interpret such ambiguous situations as the one described.

Some people might think:

"Well, I'm the first, I will choose the most comfortable place" (+, +),

and others: "They changed the time and I have forgotten because I am a muddler, others can be organised, while I can't" (–, +),

or: "Others are late, of course, and we will waste precious time for our work" (+, –),

and some "What am I doing here? I should have stayed home. What a lot of time I'm wasting with people I don't care about and who can't help me!" (–, –).

Emotional reactions are thus connected to these different representations of the event: I feel at ease while waiting for the others (+, +), I become anxious and fret (–, +), or I start accumulating resentment, so I get angry (+, –) or I experience a sense of void and desperation (–, –).

What do you say after you say hello?

A person's behaviour after the others arrive in the group, the way one says hello, and the first transactional interactions are thus activated in the ego state which will be mainly energised with the thoughts and emotions described above. The therapist will, therefore, already have a chance to observe interesting and significant differences between the participants in the first exchanges. The group begins when the people arrive, say hello, and sit down. The therapist usually arrives some minutes later, and the dynamic is activated when she takes a seat: the group time begins from that very moment. Berne said that, at the initial phase, a group member perceives the group situation as an undifferentiated whole in which only one's own slot (narcissistic slot) and the therapist's slot (transference slot) are distinguished; the others are seen as a whole from which only later other figures will be differentiated as individual figures.

Indeed, at a phase of introduction into the group, one can observe that the new member addresses only the therapist, often looks in her direction only, and does not remember the names of other group members. The new participant usually asks the therapist about the rules to be followed, and expects to receive information and support from her. An evolution can be observed when the new participant will be addressed directly by a peer and when he begins asking for information, asking questions, and openly disagreeing on some points.

The passage to the conflict phase in fact indicates a positive evolution, as the person feels sure that he belongs in that context and gives himself permission to explore his own space, his power, as well as that of others. It is as if people begin to touch each other when they begin to confront each other; being willing to exchange, being awkward in doing it, or making attempts that are sometimes awkward and sometimes aggressive to search for a contact, are extremely important experiences. Until children push, bite, or insult each other, they cannot even learn what the limit is in interaction, and how convenient it is to negotiate. Negotiating, which creates conditions to get back to playing after a fight, is the most helpful art in life, an art that needs exercising in order to be refined. Preventing children from confronting each other means leaving them completely unprepared to face the conflict that they are inevitably going to experience in relationships. If it is true that adults must not overstimulate aggressiveness or be overprotective, then it is true for the group therapist as well. She will have to intervene so that the conflict will not degenerate and lead to offensive judgements and, at the same time, cannot stop any manifestation of conflicts—albeit sometimes a little inappropriate—because this might block the participants' learning. It is very helpful to analyse in the group how conflicts begin, and, especially when their beginning is not evident, it is important to invite the participants to make the latent conflict explicit and have the members experience that it is possible to negotiate and find a constructive use for anger on a social level.

A group therapist cannot be afraid of anger or prevent group members from expressing aggressiveness, either towards each other or towards her. If she blocks this process, the group is stuck in a symbiotic dependence that is not conducive to evolution. For Berne, this is the second phase of group imago. When the group members elaborate the meaning of the conflicts, their imago becomes more and more differentiated, they have a chance to recognise others as peers, and live more experiences of exchange and projections through the exchange with them. A third phase is thus reached, in which interactions among participants increase, and psychological games among members are activated, as they proceed to a time structuring that is more and more determined by the search for strokes, deeper stimuli, and confirmation of the script. Those who enter this third phase prepare to reach deconfusion, if they are ready to accept confrontation about games and to energise the Adult in order to understand the meaning of feelings they have or roles they play in the group, just as they do in their external lives.

To the fourth phase patients bring their dreams, in which the group and the therapist are present, the deepest script issues emerge, each member works on a very deep level individually, and emotional contacts and insights are frequent, even in the exchanges among participants. It is the phase of intimacy and activity. Gestalt exercises and the analysis of dreams are helpful because the person is bringing out the Child world in which he is immersed and into which he is willing to let archaic memories and primary decisions re-emerge.

The fifth phase is the phase of elaboration of detachment, which accompanies the path to awareness of introjection of the internal Parent as a good and protective parent. It is a phase in which telling about successes at work or in one's affective life external to the group helps as a confirmation of the change that has taken place and as an encouragement to leave the nest-group.

Living the Bionian aspect of the group: the group as an organism

The path to awareness and elaboration of the imago is indeed an individual path in the group. Nonetheless, it is important for a transactional analyst to observe how the concept of imago can have a bionian application, that is, it can also be used to describe certain phases of the collective process. A group based on Berne's theory is averagely semi-open, that is, it begins with a certain number of patients (from four to eight) and then, as someone leaves the group at the end of his path, new members enter. The time in which one is in the group is thus different, and the phases of personal imago can be differentiated. However, the group sometimes seems to function as a single organism, and the model of imago can describe the experience of collective projections. The therapist can, in fact, perceive that the group is not yet structured, or that it is entering the conflict phase, or doing pastimes, or finally producing a common result until it elaborates separation.

Tuckman's model (Tuckman, 1977), which described group phases as collective phases starting from the analysis of training groups, can indeed be applied to the marathon groups—in which the number of participants is the same at the beginning and at the end—and only in part to the weekly analytical groups if we, as therapists, can keep in mind that two levels coexist: collective and individual. A mature group, for example, that is at phase four on a collective level, and in which deep experiences and dreams are being analysed, begins to indulge in the intimacy that has been acquired until one of the members announces he wants to end therapy. Someone in the group might be upset and confront the participant aggressively, telling him that he is not ready and his decision is premature. Accordingly, if the group seconds the person who is preparing to leave the group and suggests a correct perspective for the fear of the member who is afraid of separation, the group will proceed to phase five. On the other hand, if the group identifies with the fear expressed by the participant who is anguished by the ghost of separation, it might regress to the phase of games, phase three or even phase two, the phase of conflict. It is very important for a group therapist to follow, on the one hand, the collective process influenced by the emerging of various levels of leadership and, on the other, the participants' personal situations. In fact, the latter never completely coincide with the collective process if the people are healthy enough and the group is not pathologically psychoticising.

The psychoticising group is one in which everyone is convinced they feel the same emotions and live in a condition of collective fusion. This does not happen if the therapist is trained and the group is supervised, as it always ought to be.

A therapist cannot begin a therapy group unless during her training she has personally experienced the group as a patient. Indeed, the intensity of the emotions to be dealt with, and the complexity of the data to be analysed, could not even be perceived by someone who has not deeply experienced them personally.

In TA, the focus of group treatment is the development of the imago of the participants, which is required in order to achieve the contractual objective. The group analysis is helpful as a background and comparison between the individual's level and the level of the collective organism. Such a comparison is also a helpful element in making a diagnosis: for instance, a patient who denies the perception of conflict when everyone else feels involved in it shows us how isolated that patient is and how his defences work, just as much as a patient who remains alone in the conflict while everyone else has moved towards more intimate exchanges indicates that he is afraid of being close to others and establishing a bond with them.

Alessio's case

An only child from a working class family, he begins therapy because he has been referred by the seventh psychiatrist who has followed him.

He is twenty-eight; he introduces himself by saying that his father died eight years ago, he lives with his mother, and works in the company where his father worked. He has been having treatment for depression since he was six; he has had periods of health alternating with long periods of distress, which have always been treated psychopharmacologically. When he began therapy, he was being treated with anxiolytics and antidepressants for depression with panic attacks. He had previously been diagnosed with childhood depression, then school phobia, and generalised anxiety disorder.

His resources:

Alessio has been working and studying since he was twenty: he is a worker and works eight hours a day, then he studies at university. He has chosen the civil service. He has had three girlfriends and quite a satisfactory sex life. He reads and he is politically active.

His difficulties:

He has not graduated yet, and he suffers a lot before exams.

He cannot have long-term relationships because he feels suffocated. He is obsessed by the thought that his mother will die, makes her undergo medical check-ups, and does not want to leave his mother's house. He is a lonely person, he gets bored, he does not really have a social life. He thinks he will be unable to continue working and that he will end up alone in a psychiatric hospital. I bring Alessio into the group after fifteen individual sessions, in which he is mainly in his Adapted Child and complains. I find out, however, that although he introduces himself as a "psychiatric patient", he hardly ever followed the therapies prescribed, and never told the doctors, although he was supposed to.

Alessio's first period in the groups

Provisional imago: he does not want to enter. He perceives and describes himself as different from everybody. In fact, he does not look anyone in the eye, he is on his own, he does not even listen, he is often distracted. When he asks to speak, he turns to me, the therapist, and says: "I want to tell you …". He ignores the others and only looks at me.

Intervention: unconditioned strokes, emphasising adaptive behaviours, invitation to establish a playful contact with the others, confronting the incongruity (you come to the group, but you only speak to me: shall I translate for the others?).

Alessio's second phase in the group

Provisionally adapted imago: he is encouraged by the other members of the group to speak and exchange ideas with others; Giulia accuses him of being there without a role and of not being interested in others. Alessio is afraid of such direct stimuli, but he likes being addressed directly. He quarrels with some members of the group, jokes with others; the moments of contact with the members increase.

Intervention: emphasis, specifications to stress the value of the energy of the Rebel Child and the new experiences of exchange and contact.

Alessio's third phase in the group

Operative imago: a period of intense exchange begins. He asks me, as a therapist, "What do you think about me?", asks for confirmations, he plays "Wooden leg" and "Poor me" (Berne, 1964). After the summer break, he does not call me by name, he calls me "Doctor", as if he were seeing me for the first time. He is no longer on first name terms and asks for an individual session because he feels "terrible". In the confrontations in the group, he declares that he is angry because he felt he has been "abandoned" during the summer, while he actually lives in his own house and he is doing pretty well. The comments from the group are affective and ironical: "Look, you're smarter than you think."

Intervention: analysis of games and subsequently confrontations, emphasis and specifications of new, realistic, adaptive behaviours, then illustration, confirmation, and crystallisations.

Alessio's fourth phase in the group

Secondarily adapted imago: period rich in experiences and intimacy in the group. Alessio feels part of the group, is nourished by the group's affection, he always sits close to someone, touches the others and lets them touch him. He speaks addressing every member, calls them by name, tells them about his difficulties and achievements. He ends therapy after four years, having been free from medication and psychiatrists for three years; he has graduated, is autonomous from his mother, has a steady love relationship and a group of friends.

Interventions: in some moments each phase is reanalysed in micro-sequences, interpretations and crystallisations enable Alessio to let the awareness and energy of the reparative here and now leave a sediment and stratify. The therapist is, for him, his mother; the group represents the world. The mother-therapist was for Alessio a dangerous and entangling place for relationships, in which he was drowned by evil fantasies and childish demands. Growing up implied loneliness and abandonment. In Alessio's experience as a child there were no brothers or sisters or positive friends. The group becomes the world and a training place, a nurturing and nourishing place, but at the same time a more realistic place to which to adapt himself. The group reactions represented the main factor for change for Alessio, providing him with new attachment patterns and opportunities. My initial intuition was: this child is too lonely, he cannot play with others, he needs to learn to play, to touch and be touched.

Terry's case

Terry is a woman aged forty-five; she is a clerk. When I meet her, she has a husband and two children—Giulia, thirteen years old and Luca, nine years old. She began therapy when her daughter presented worrying adolescent symptoms of parental refusal, with violent threats to her brother and self-destructive behaviours.

Terry would say: "I'm here for my daughter", but then, every time she spoke, she spoke about herself. Her husband and her son were never part of her stories. She had a deep sense of guilt about Giulia: "I nearly killed her." When Giulia was four, her brother having been born a short time before, Terry was responsible for her daughter being in a coma due to a very high fever because she refused to take her to hospital, until her husband took the child from her. "Now she wants to kill me", she says in the first interview. The therapeutic approach of the team for three years was to follow Giulia with both a pharmacological treatment and psychotherapy, and to follow her parents in a support therapy whose purpose was to reinforce their parental competences. As Giulia's behaviours became less worrying, and her parents managed to deal with both of their children, we accepted Terry's request to begin individual psychotherapy with TA. Giulia attends high school, is politically active, and has a boyfriend. She has completed the pharmacological treatment and is still seeing a psychotherapist; she will stop when she is seventeen and start again out of choice when she is twenty. Luca finishes lower secondary school, starts high school, and little by little finds his own space in his family. The father is the one who makes decisions about the relationship with the children, and he has a constructive, important role in Giulia's therapy too. The children tend to rely on him more than on their mother because Terry is very little involved in the decisions that concern them. Terry comes from a middle-class family, and her mother categorically rejects the children, whom she has never hugged and with whom she shakes hands as if they were strangers (she seems to have a serious narcissistic disorder and to propose an avoidant attachment). Terry does not remember much about her father. Terry is apparently cold, with a gelid anger; only Giulia's emotional impetus seems to touch her. There is not enough room for everyone in her family of origin: her mother takes up all the space. At work and in her family, Terry feels as if she is not there: "I'm like a shadow. I don't decide anything. I don't say what I think, I don't say what I want." However, as her husband declared in the therapy for the parental couple: "We really are all subjugated to your will, we only do what you want us to do." Terry is introduced into a group after a period of individual treatment. We are currently at the final phase of her treatment, and the following reflections come from an exchange between Terry and me about her path in the group.

Terry's first phase in the group

Provisional imago: she does not want to enter, she feels different from the others and defines herself as such. In fact, she does not look at anyone, she sits aside, she does not even listen, she blushes if someone asks her something. When she asks to speak, she turns to me, her therapist, and says "I'm going to tell you ..." She ignores the others and only looks at me. She clearly shows that she is not listening to the others and that she gets annoyed if she cannot speak. She agrees to listen to the others—if they do not take too much time, and only provided that she has had a chance to speak herself. She would like to divide up the time by assigning just a few minutes to each of the others to speak.

Intervention: unconditioned positive recognition, emphasis on adaptive behaviours, invitations to establish a playful contact with others, then confrontation about incongruity (you come to the group but you only speak to me: shall I translate for the others?).

Terry's experience: "At the beginning I'm very curious, and I'm attracted by novelties. S. bothers me because she speaks too much, what she says is no use to me, she deprives me of my space. K. also bothers me, because she is not sincere and when she speaks she deprives me of my space. When I speak I like it, I calm down, I feel I'm really there, but at the same time I feel guilty because I'm depriving someone of their space. Meanwhile, immersed in this uneasiness, worried about not having enough space, I don't enjoy the novelty, I don't participate and unless I have previously spoken, I can't understand anything of what the others say."

Second phase

Provisionally adapted imago: she starts complaining because there is not enough space for everyone. She would like the time for speaking to be equally shared. She cries (out of anger, she will say) if there is no time for her. She wants to be seen by me, the therapist, and if she is not explicitly asked to speak, she threatens to quit. She fights with some in the group, jokes around with others, the moments of contact increase.

Interventions: emphasis, specifications to stress the value of the energy of the Rebel Child and the new experiences of exchange and contact.

Terry's experience: "It bothers me that each member of the group, including the therapist, always sits in the same seat. It particularly bothers me that K. got the armchair. I would like, once in a while, to sit in E.'s [therapist] armchair and the places to be rearranged. It bothers me that we start late because of E. [therapist], and I feel relieved when someone in the group is missing. The fewer, the better. Maybe this is what I want most, so it is more likely that there is space for me."

Significant changes: "After never-ending doubts and second thoughts I decide to attend a residential training group in the summer, I take my own space. I join a drama group and I begin to express myself. I feel part of a small group of colleagues."

Third phase

Operative imago: a period of intense exchanges begins. She asks me, the therapist, "What do you see in me?", she asks for confirmations, wants to know how important she is for me. She expresses competitive behaviors, the games she activates in the group are "Schlemiel" and "If it weren't for you". She asks for individual interviews, then compares group therapy with drama experiences and considers therapy a less valuable experience if compared with drama, as in a competition (it is more helpful than you). In confrontations in the group, her anger emerges because she does not feel as if she is a protagonist and she does not feel she is being sufficiently helped, although she actually receives a lot of strokes. The comments from the group are affective and ironical: "Look, you're still with us!"

Interventions: analysis of games and then confrontations, emphasis and specifications of new behaviours, realistic, adaptive, then illustration, confirmation, and crystallisations.

Terry's experience: "Moving to a new study [the group moved to a larger study] meets my need to have an armchair of my own. I take it. I like sitting in the same seat, I like that place to be mine. I'm still critical about E. [therapist] I'm not sure she is the right person for me. I keep an emotional distance from her and I don't feel she is friendly to me. I think what I'm doing with her is not enough, so I keep going to the training courses I started, and I take up a therapy based on spontaneous movement. It seems that these three things together are helping me. I would like, also in the group with E., to have experiences of exchange, in pairs, in threes, all together, I would like to create a relationship with the other members of the group. I'm critical about the 'speak one at a time' policy, one can start only after the other has finished—this way there is no interaction. I would like to share what I've experienced outside the group, but I don't. I need someone to give me permission to do it, it would take time and I don't know if the others are interested. I just let E. get the message 'You're not doing enough'. I express the idea to quit therapy, and I'm glad that E. won't let me go. I begin feeling present and part of the group. I always need E. to give me permission to assert myself and to express what I'm feeling. At the same time, I feel more comfortable when there is only C. [co-therapist] to conduct the group. Meanwhile, thanks to my drama experience, I start being visible, and I occupy my own place on the sofa and in the group. I feel under the spotlight."

Significant changes: "I find myself the protagonist in a theatre production. I find myself facing the fact that not everyone likes me, and I accept that. I'm perfectly comfortable when the group becomes smaller, I feel surrounded by the intimacy that has been created. My daughter leaves our house and goes to live on her own. From inside me emerges the idea that there is something buried down deep and removed."

Fourth phase

Secondarily adapted imago: a period rich in experiences and intimacy in the group. Terry feels part of the group, she is close to the others, looks at them, and lets others look at her. She speaks and addresses everyone, calls the others by name, talks about her achievements and her difficulties. She often brings her dreams and her drawings, in which there is always the group and a wall falling down.

Interventions: at some moments, we analyse all the phases in microsequences, interpretation prevails, and ancient memories of childhood and ancient traumas re-emerge.

Terry's experience: "I'm closer to my husband, and I wish to meet him. I'm not so uncomfortable about his anger, or the thought that he is going to get angry at me and doesn't understand me. I feel fine when he is here too. New people are introduced in the group, and this attracts me, rather than bothering me. I can participate even if I never speak in a whole meeting. In the drama group, I always express my anger. I'm more and more aware that for me the relationship with others is a fight for power, 'either you or me …' [she cries as she says this and marks the sheet with a tear]. Either I prevail, and judge the other, don't listen to him, or I abandon the field, and get revenge through emotional distance. There isn't space for me and the other together. I feel the need to inquire deeply into my relationship with my parents, with my husband and with E."

Significant changes: "I spend a week alone with my husband and I'm perfectly at ease. We talk, and he says he feels fine too."

Currently: fifth phase

Terry can prepare herself to leave the group, she must be free to take the time she needs to separate. She is coming for some individual sessions to re-elaborate her path, and then she talks about that in the group. Commenting on Terry's path, I reflect on the fact that I proposed that she enter the group quite early because individual treatment was more difficult for her, she had a negative transference full of cold anger towards the therapist and she would probably have quit therapy. The mother-therapist was for Terry an unknown and feared place for relationship, from which she escaped. One of her first memories is dancing alone in the living room. She remembers the rooms, the house, not her mother's presence. Her father, who was more affective, has been suppressed from her memory. Growing up meant freeing herself from an oppressive absence-presence (her mother was a painter and filled their house with her paintings). In her childhood experiences there weren't any positive friends, brothers, or sisters, although she does have two brothers—but with them, she hardly had a relationship. The group becomes a world-training place, a nourishing and nurturing place, but at the same time a more realistic place to adapt to, a place to be feared because there is no friendly, welcoming place to go back to. Terry had run away from her family when she was twenty, as soon as she had had a chance. The group relationship offers her new attachments and new opportunities, and they are the main factor for change for Terry.

My initial intuition had been: this woman will not be able to be a mother unless she is accepted as a child and her trauma is healed. "I am a bad mother who didn't want her children, who nearly killed them and would want to get rid of them now." In another episode, she remembers that she had to cross a road with her two children; each of them was on a different bicycle. She sent them forward and remained on the sidewalk, without protecting them, and then felt guilty at the thought that a car could hit them. Her mother is a bad mother too, she never hugs her children and always shakes hands with them as if they were some strangers she had just been introduced to. The therapist is perceived as bad, too, and Terry does not feel wanted: "Perhaps you're not the right person to take care of me", Terry would say to me. The sentence: "There isn't space enough for you and me" always resounds inside Terry, and it means: for me and my mother, for me and my daughter, for me and my husband, for me and my son, for me and the group. "Therapist, and what about you, have you got a place for me? The group can be a welcoming womb: you and I in the warmth of other people close to us, it can be the place where we see ourselves mirrored in others, where we learn to express our emotions and to be close to the parental figures." It is to the group that Terry brings a lot of dreams, elaborates the deepest experiences, and then asks for individual sessions to reanalyse the emotional material that the group so richly aroused. The important dreams say that in this place anguish ends and a bag is found that was always lost.

CHAPTER ELEVEN

Using dreams in psychotherapy

Everything begins with Freud

Freud's hypothesis was that dreams originated from the phantasmatic representation of a wish (sexual or aggressive) that was censured by the oneiric work through a masking process. The latter produced a "manifest" content more acceptable for one's conscience than the "latent" content that contained the deeper message. This process of censorship had a defensive purpose and allowed the dreamer to gratify some impulses without disturbing the dreamer. Thus, in Freud's view, the dream was used to discharge an impulse connected with a wish so that it did not represent a danger for the subject's conscience. "My procedure is not so convenient as the popular decoding method, which translates any given piece of a dream's content by a fixed key. I, on the contrary, am prepared to find that the same piece of content may conceal a different meaning when it occurs in various people or in various contexts" (Freud, 1900a, p. 105). Freud was the first academic who dealt with dreams and maintained that the interpretation of dreams was up to the dreamer; we will later see how this process is actually a relational process between patient and therapist.

Dreams are a psychic phenomenon. It is a dreamer's production and expression, which is, however, incomprehensible. "What do you do when I make a statement you do not understand? You ask for an explanation, do you not? Why may we not do the same thing here, ask the dreamer to give us the meaning of his dream? (Freud, 1916b, p. 101).

The fundamental difference, therefore, between this method and the previous ones lies in the fact that the analyst does not act as a priest who has an *a priori* understanding of the meaning of the dream. The dreamer himself holds the hidden meaning of the oneiric scene, which, in fact, we are told by Freud, is his own "production" and "expression". Now, "the dreamer always says he knows nothing". Actually, Freud goes on, the dreamer "does know what his dream means: only he does not know that he knows it and for that reason thinks he does not know it" (Freud, 1916b, p. 101).

Thus, Freud introduces the idea of an internal division in the subject between a conscious belief not to know and unconscious knowledge that conscience knows nothing about. Freud invites us to "separate the dream into its elements" so as to "carry on the investigation of each element separately."

"If I ask someone to tell me what occurs to him in response to a particular element of a dream, I am asking him to surrender himself to free association, *while keeping an idea in mind as a starting point*. This calls for a special attitude of the attention, which is quite different from reflection and which exclude reflection" (Freud, 1916b, p. 106).

This is the method of free association, which led Freud to abandon hypnosis and discover psychoanalysis. In order to avoid misunderstandings, I want to be clear about the meaning of the word "free" in the phrase "free association".

Freud's dream about Irma

Freud says that in the summer of 1895 he treated a young woman, Irma, who was a family friend of his. It is known that in the psychotherapeutic field, a friendly relationship between doctor and patient may deeply upset the process of therapy. According to Freud, this therapy was only partially successful and, even though young Irma did solve her problem of hysterical anguish, she nonetheless did not recover from her somatic symptoms. "Analytic treatment" thus definitely did not solve the problem. However, we have to consider that Freud was at the beginning of his psychoanalytic discoveries.

One day, a colleague and friend of Freud's, Otto, told him he had seen Irma. Freud asked him if she seemed fine and the young man's answer—"She's better, but not quite well"—greatly irritated Freud. That same night, he wrote, almost as if he were justifying himself, a description of the clinical case of Irma's sickness, which he would deliver to doctor M., an authority in the clinical field.

That night, he had this dream:

> I take her to the window and looked down her throat, and she showed signs of recalcitrance, like a woman with artificial dentures. I thought to myself that there was really no need for her to do that. She then opened her mouth properly and on the right I found a big white patch; at another place I saw extensive whitish grey scabs upon some remarkable curly structures which were evidently modelled on the turbinal bones of the nose.
>
> I at once called in Dr. M., and he repeated the examination and confirmed it ... Dr. M. looked quite different from usual; he was very pale, he walked with a limp and his chin was clean-shaven ...
>
> My friend Otto was now standing beside her as well, and my friend Leopold was percussing her through her bodice and saying: "She has a dull area low down on the left". He also indicated that a portion of the skin on the left shoulder was infiltrated. (I noticed this, just as he did, in spite of her dress) ... Dr. M. said: "There's no doubt it's an infection, but no matter; dysentery will supervene, and the toxin will be eliminated"... We were directly aware too of the origin of the infection. Not long before, when she was feeling unwell, my friend Otto had given her an injection of a preparation of propyl ... propyls ... propionic acid ... trimethylamin. (and I saw before me the formula for this printed in heavy type) ... Injections of that sort ought not to be made so thoughtlessly ... And probably the syringe had not been clean. (Freud, 1900a, p. 107)

Freud's auto-analysis:

> *The hall—numerous guests, whom we were receiving.* We were spending that summer at Bellevue, a house standing by itself on one of the hills adjoining the Kahlenberg. The house had formerly been

designed as a place of entertainment, and its reception-rooms were in consequence unusually lofty and hall-like. It was at Bellevue that I had the dream, a few days before my wife's birthday. On the previous day my wife had told me that she expected that a number of friends, including Irma, would be coming out to visit us as for her birthday. My dream was, thus, anticipating this occasion: it was my wife's birthday, and a number of guests, including Irma, were been received by us in the large hall at Bellevue.

I reproached Irma for not having accepted my "solution"; I said, "If you still get pains, it's your own fault". I might have said this to her in waking life; I may actually have done so it. [...] I noticed, however, that the words which I spoke to Irma in the dream showed that I was specially anxious not to be responsible for the pains which she still had. If they were her fault, they could not be mine. Could it be that the purpose of the dream lay in this direction?

Irma's complaint—pains in her throat, abdomen, and stomach; it was choking her. Pains in the stomach were among my patient's symptoms, but were not very prominent; she complained more of feelings of nausea and disgust. Pains in the throat and abdomen and constriction of the throat played scarcely any part in her illness. I wondered why I decided upon this choice of symptoms in the dream but could not think of an explanation at the moment [...].

I was alarmed at the idea that I had missed an organic illness. This, as may well be believed, is a perpetual source of anxiety to a specialist whose practice is almost limited to neurotic patients and who is in the habit of attributing to hysteria a great number of symptoms which other physicians treat as organic. On the other hand, a faint doubt crept into my mind—from where, I could not tell—that my alarm was not entirely genuine. If Irma's pains had an organic basis, once again I could not be held responsible for curing them; my treatment only set out to get rid of *hysterical* pains. It occurred to me, in fact, that I was actually *wishing* that there had been a wrong diagnosis; for, if so, the blame for my lack of success would also have been got rid of. (Freud, 1900a, pp. 108–109)

The conclusion reached by the psychoanalyst is that that dream intended to punish and humiliate both Irma and his friend and colleague Otto, as well as Doctor M. He got revenge on Irma by exchanging her for a friend of hers in the dream, on Otto by blaming him for an evidently dangerous injection, and on Doctor M. by having him express an inappropriate opinion from a scientific point of view about dysentery as a remedy for intoxication. Besides, the dream lifted Freud from responsibility for Irma's conditions, as it showed that they were due to other factors. The dream may thus represent a defensive pleading and the realisation of the aggressive and competitive wishes of Freud himself.

For Freud, dreams are the royal road to the unconscious, and the dynamic unconscious was for him one of the three great scientific discoveries that lowered man's status, the third after those of Copernicus and Darwin. The dream represents a disguised version of a wish. The defence mechanisms used to create a dream are:

Condensation: a single image contains several wishes, impulses and feelings.

Displacement: emotional intensity associated with a person is displaced to another person in order for the emotion to be more acceptable.

Symbolic representation: a concrete image substitutes as a symbol feelings and objects loaded with meaning (e.g., a flower for female genitals or a house for the mind).

Secondary elaboration: the bizarre components of the dream are reorganised in a story characterised by a little rationality.

After Freud

The main object of the latent content of the dream is the latent intersystemic conflict. Jung (1916), Adler (1936), and Fromm (1951) are just some of the authors who carried on studying dreams in the psychoanalytic field. The progressive aspects, the problem solving and self-reparative function of dreams are highlighted.

W. R. D. Fairbairn (1952) states that dreams are representations of "endopsychic situations" on which the person who dreams is blocked (fixation points) and they often include some attempt to overcome the situation itself, as in the case of fears, conflicts, or traumatic experiences.

In self psychology, H. Kohut (1977) hypothesises that when the self is threatened by a state of fragmentation or dissolution, the function of the dream is to restore the self (self-state dreams). This subsequently implies a high cognitive functioning of the dream, whereas the importance of the defensive function decreases.

In non-psychoanalytical fields, some of the new studies about dreams are: the psycho-physiology of sleep and dream; research on the contents of dreams; cognitive psychology.

Important: research on REM sleep and mental activity during the dream have an essential role in affect regulation, memory consolidation, information elaboration, and stress adaptation.

Dreaming is a complex mental process which has an adaptive function. According to Freud, dreams and symptoms followed the primary process (the archaic process of thinking in which energy seeks immediate discharge according to the pleasure principle). In the secondary process, energy is retained and its discharge is delayed.

Fosshage's writings (1983) are particularly helpful and close to a TA view of the dream: the main function of dreams is to organise data.

The condensation, displacement, and symbolisation principles imply organisation and structure. Primary process is thus nowadays seen as the mental functioning which uses visual images and other sensorial images affectively connoted so as to carry out a function of general integration and synthesis. They are complementary ways to learn, to respond and organise the experiential world. Both processes are operative and they intertwine in day and night mental activity. Through the dream, the dreamer looks for new perceptive prospectives, tries to elaborate the experience, and identify new models of behaviour. For Hartmann (1973), dreams have a semi-therapeutic function and for Greenberg (Greenberg & Perlman, 1993) a problem-solving one.

Cerebral activity is intensified during REM sleep.

REM sleep increases when we learn new things.

REM sleep contributes to increasing memory. Predominant mental activity in REM sleep is full of affective images.

Dreams foster the structuring of neural networks and memory images.

Dreams have functions of restoration and preservation.

Mental activity helps regulate and preserve self-esteem, attachment, sexual experiences, exploration, self-confidence, and aversion.

For example: if during the day we have not had the chance to express our anger for something that we perceived as threatening, in the dream we may get the situation right. In sleep, as in waking, a usual mental scheme can be re-established and reinforced, even though it is problematic.

A dream can be used to reaffirm a negative self-vision of inadequacy that is more familiar and causes less anxiety than the object-self. For example, if my being successful is threatening to the other person, I might dream that I redefine it in a less daunting way so as to prevent envy or affective losses. The nightmare reveals a remarkable failure in dealing with a particularly anxiety-inducing stimulus or a conflict. For example, the evolutive attempts at change can directly contrast with the attempts to preserve the current psychological organisation.

Fosshage on the content of dreams

Dreams more directly reveal the dreamer's immediate concerns through affects, metaphors, and themes.

Fromm (1951, p. 12) speaks of symbolic language as a forgotten language, not a language that disguises, but rather as "language in which we express inner experience as if it were a sensory experience".

One's defenses must preserve their self-cohesion and in dreams they appear in the form of aversiveness.

There is no distinction between manifest and latent content, as the content of dreams is revelatory in itself—although this is not immediately apparent.

A person chooses images not for the purpose of disguising but for their immediate evocative power, a characteristic that facilitates thinking and communicating.

Thus, the analytic work helps to clarify the meaning and translate it into comprehensible language.

To understand a dream's themes and metaphors the person must accurately describe his dream experience, associations, and resonance with the dream's affects, and the analyst must enquire about the dream and its waking connection.

For example, "I" in the dream indicates the person who dreams, the image-objects represent the dreamer's image of the other person. However, investigation may reveal that some aspects of the one person are projected on to the other person.

Not all dreams are significant. Some, like the non-REM ones, may simply be concerned with some real aspects of daily life, such as finishing a paper or mowing the lawn. This lifts from both the analyst and the patient the pointless task of looking for a meaning where there is none.

Traditionally, we think that lack of clarity is due to defensive activity. The former, however, can indeed reflect defensive processes, but also the mental process itself.

Fosshage's principles to work with dreams

The analytic situation is an intersubjective field in which analyst and patient create a system of reciprocal interactions and influence.

Analytic interaction therefore affects the patient's dreams, the selection of dreams to be reported to the analyst, and how the dreams are reported.

First technical principle: listen very carefully to the patient's experience during the dream: use of the empathic mode of perception.

Second technical principle: amplify the patient's experience within the dream. For example, "How did you feel when this thing happened in the dream? What were you experiencing?" Not "What do you associate with the dream?"

Third technical principle: dream imagery is not to be translated, but is to be understood in its metaphorical and thematic content. Every image is like a word in a sentence and sequences of images are like sentences and paragraphs that tell a story.

Fourth technical principle: connect the dream experience and waking life. For example, a positive dream that confirms the dreamer's intellectual capacities can either consolidate waking feelings or have a restorative function in the face of self-doubt.

Fifth technical principle: the interpretation of the dream is shaped by the patient and the analyst together. Every dream the patient reports to the analyst has a transferential meaning; the meaning lies in its content, or else the process of communicating the dream carries the primary meaning for the analytic relationship.

Sixth technical principle: if a relational pattern is repetitive, this pattern needs to be identified and connected to the patient's waking life. The same pattern may be occurring in the analytic relationship as well—and in this case the transferential meaning is conveyed—or it may not. The content of the dream is not directly linked to the transference, unless the analyst herself appears in the dream.

Seventh technical principle: dreams are useful in the psychotherapy of any patient. The analysis of a dream never creates disturbance. A comprehensive vision of ourselves and of our life is sometimes captured in a dream and it can be fully appreciated only if we listen to the dream itself.

The clinical case narrated by Fosshage:

> A very intelligent thirty-nine-year-old woman. She grew up as the perfect child, and her parents had great expectations for her. She had become a very cold person. She had been sexually abused by her brother and by a neighbour.
>
> While she was being followed by a therapist for her paranoid fears and suicidal fantasies, she had been admitted to hospital.
>
> The dream: a village on a hill. Wintertime, snow; it's quiet. I know I am the village, nonetheless I am also watching it from above.
>
> Fear. The village is in a state of apparent death. It's frozen, completely still.
>
> After twenty years, the village unfreezes. I find myself walking in it, I can see some soil emerge from the snow.
>
> Analysis of the dream: the twenty-year sleep began when the patient was about nineteen, when she met her husband. She was detached, pretty, and feminine, just as in the first part of the dream she described. Then, when she is in the hospital, she is terrified of her feelings, and becomes frozen just as in the dream. The unfreezing process begins when, in therapy, she returns to her experience, more vital and livelier.

Transactional Analysis of dreams

Berne (1968) writes: "It is probable that dreams assist in healing the mind after emotional wounds and distressing experiences".

In TA we say that the dreamer himself writes the script. What is meant is that the dream is constructed mainly with the language of the Child ego state, according to the logic, the emotional intensity, and the decisional choices of the Little Professor (the nucleus of the Adult ego state, called A1), the state of mind that decides on the psychological script. Having access to dreams is thus fundamental in order to discover the unconscious parts of the script and to reveal to the patient and to the therapist how the "child mind"—which has so much power both over the choices made to survive and emotional decisions—works.

Irene's dream

I'm at your house, there are a lot of people and I come towards you [therapist].

Some purebred attack dogs are arriving.

You let them in! I shout: what the hell are you doing?

I stretch out my arm to protect myself and a dog bites me.

I think: he wanted revenge because I had delicately slapped you on the face.

I am resigned to the dog's biting me all the time.

I can't get free of it, it's dragging me and I must follow it.

The front door looks like cardboard, outside there are some Moroccan people who are trying to enter and I wake up in anguish.

Analysis of the dream. Irene is attending group therapy: She is very aggressive towards the other members, when she speaks she is as aggressive as a dog that wants to bite someone and she is very biting in her observations. She is afraid that someone might "bite" her and that the therapist won't protect her, that the therapist will leave her alone and she will be led away by her rage, her attack dog. The biting dog also represents the repeating of depression and dysphoria.

Second dream Irene reported in the group. After the session of group therapy:

There's a child that doesn't look like me and it's a boy, accompanied by a woman.

He sits down so he can put his rollerskates on.

Then, a man, who is my father, says: Speak, speak.

And the woman says: Can't you see he has lost his power of speech?! He has to get used to the new condition. Then I say: Try the roller blades, they are faster!

Analysis of the dream:

For me, being depressed is like losing the power of speech. In order not to feel emotions, I'm always in a hurry and I do a lot of things. I can't find the words to say how I feel. I feel like a child, not a woman.

In dynamic psychotherapy, dreams become a moment of intense communication between therapist and patient. When a patient begins to remember his dreams and to report them in therapy sessions, he is trying to communicate something relevant to himself and to the therapist through the cryptic and dense language of dreams.

According to the underlying logic of the treatment I am describing, a dream is a message that the patient sends to himself. The help he requires from the therapist is the decoding of the message itself, which is sometimes incomprehensible and often comes with intense emotions—mostly anguish. Rarely is a dream accompanied by pleasant sensations.

However, whoever listens to the dream is like an archaeologist in front of the ruins of a pyramid in the desert. Approaching a world of symbols and broken memories belonging to someone we do not know requires tactfulness.

A correct attitude for a therapist is, therefore, exploration.

Second, you must be aware that you are dealing with an imagistic language. As a consequence, just as with a painting or a surreal film, you cannot expect only one possible interpretation. In other words, you cannot expect the dream to correspond to a second order linear logic.

An image is evocative, it has the power to recall emotions, and contains multiple meanings, it is closer to symbols than prose.

The vocabulary of the dream world is thus the language of symbols and images, poetic intenseness, metaphors, and analogies.

It is a Child language, often forgotten and which has become inaccessible to the adult man, who is no longer able to perceive unaffectedly the message that comes from inside.

Anthropological studies are the best way to prepare oneself for listening to a dream. The ancient native Australian civilisation describes dream-time as a time in the archaic epoch when human beings lived in harmony with the cosmos and had a power that has now been lost. Observing archeological finds, researchers have established that native Australians have lived in Australia for forty thousand years. Someone has even hypothesised that the native Australians' presence on the Australian continent dates back one hundred and fifty thousand years, although there is no evidence to demonstrate this for certain. Native Australians, on the other hand, claim that they have always inhabited Australia, since dream-time, the time of creation.

Dream-time is the time in which the Ancestor Creators, also known as Ancestor Spirits, or Ancestors, came to the Earth in order to create. The Ancestors were very powerful beings, and they could create or destroy, turn themselves into anything they wished, change the shape of the land, and heal. Following a dream of creation, they shaped the land and created every living species. Once their work was done, they turned themselves into elements of the creation in the sky or on earth, and retired to some particularly beautiful places that still vibrate with their powers.

Thanks to the Ancestors' work, dreaming on earth was represented during dream-time. Thus, dreaming and dream-time are the same thing, and this is why native Australians make no distinction between them. Being an exact reproduction of dreaming, dream-time is, in fact, dreaming. A dream, for this ancient civilisation, is thus a creative activity. Such an interesting reflection may lead us to another very interesting issue.

Why do we dream and what are dreams for?

The dream is probably a problem-solving activity of our mind and, at the same time, a precious defragmenting process of our internal computer.

The dream is therefore a message meant to provide indications, solutions, paths to face a problem our mind is dealing with and that deeply absorbs our emotions.

Berne (1968) wrote: "It is a common error to suppose that *finding out* the meaning of the dream is the important thing. This is not so. The meanings must be *felt*, not merely understood, for the interpretation to have any effect in changing the underlying Id tensions, which is the purpose of the procedure" (Berne, 1968, p. 117).

Working with dreams in therapy is useful because it leads the patient to confront emotions and contents that upset him, to become more familiar with his inner monsters, to learn to listen to his inner advisor (the Little Professor) who is trying to do his best to survive.

In particular, in psychodynamic therapy, the dream also implies a deeper analysis of the script, as if the patient, after an individual or group therapy session, kept striving to find a new balance, attempting to redecide his script through tests and mistakes.

If the therapist thinks that a little, intuitive internal therapist, who acts within dreams to find solutions and unveil enigmas, is activated in the patient, this means that both therapy and the protagonists of analysis during the day are supported during the night-time. The dreamer is the night-time researcher who is our ally in our task and subsequently a precious and unique aid in the understanding and changing process the patient wishes to accomplish—despite the fears that change implies.

Marco, twenty-five years old

He suffers from panic attacks, insomnia, depression, and hypochondria. He over-indulges in cannabis. He studies philosophy, he is a brilliant student but he has not graduated yet. He lives with his father. His mother died of cancer when he was fifteen, and he later found out that she had been affected by breast cancer during her pregnancy and that over the years she had had several recurrences she did not tell him about. Marco started over-indulging in cannabis and alcohol after his mother's death. He is in conflict with his father. Marco blames him for not telling him about his mother's illness. However, he sleeps in his father's bed and thinks he cannot leave him alone.

Marco's dreams (after attending therapy for six months):

1. I undergo a heart examination. I show the result to my cousin, who is an anaesthetist, and he says that I have arrhythmia. I feel like I'm having a panic attack.

   I quarrel with my father because he criticises me; he always has a critical and discouraging attitude. My mum is there also. We are on a horse-drawn carriage. Dad is outside the carriage, and I call him all sort of names, I wish death upon him. He says: It's too much, I'm not coming with you.

   Then we go away in the carriage and he follows, walking.

   Mum is always the same in all my dreams, and she is always silent. We get home and then my father and I start quarreling again.

2. I was with my parents, both of them, I was coming home from a psychotherapy session. I went to the car and they were speaking. My father said: "It would have been better if I had died" and my mother replied: "It would have been better if I had died as a child."

   I listened, I was angry and I reacted: "Fuck the two of you, screw you and your fucking depression that made me be depressed too."

   Mum was hurt and dad got angry. I packed and left the house.

Marco starts dreaming about his mother after he has shown me a letter that she had written him before dying and that his aunt gave him after his mother's death. Marco was desperate, but he had not had a chance to be angry at his mother, nor did he have the possibility to speak to her.

Only his father was there to deal with the anger of this adolescent who was hurt so badly. His father, though, was so sad that he could not counter and restrain Marco's destructive rage.

When these dreams begin, Marco has stopped drinking, has cut down on his use of cannabis, and he finally starts talking about his mother during the therapy.

As for the dream of the carriage, he will say that in real life he has always been closer to his mother than to his father and that the carriage somehow stands for this special relationship. The carriage may recall the bride and groom, as in a fairy tale, but also a funeral. Marco let himself die, as his mother did, so he could be with her. He is in competition with his father to sit next to his mother—to show who is suffering the most.

In his second dream, Marco tries to separate himself from his parents, and he acknowledges them as a couple after the psychotherapy session. In the dream they are talking and he gets angry, tries to put a distance between him and their story of death, packs and leaves. His mother speaks to him in this dream for the first time. She used to be silent before.

Nella

> First dream: I am at Bar Sport with the students of my school; it's summertime, the weather is sunny. I'd like some cheese, but there is none left, I'm quite happy to have some flat bread, I'm fine. I come back home, and my cat looks at me with her extremely sweet black and white muzzle. Suddenly, her belly opens and bit by bit it dissolves, the entrails and the intestines come out, they are bright white and sticky. She keeps looking at me, I'm desperate, my cat is dying, she eats her entrails, her body fades away and only her head remains.

Interpretation: the cat stands for Nella and her conflict between her motherhood (she has had four children in seven years) and her job—she is an entrepreneur and a researcher. In her dream, the cat eats its bright white entrails and only her head remains there. That is how Nella feels when she starts therapy. After dedicating years to her children, she wants to take care of something else, to abandon them. Her children protest, want her to be there; in particular, her firstborn is distressed and she wants him to attend psychotherapy.

> Second dream: I'm taking a pill to treat a fibroma that might have been a cancer. My skin is smooth, while in the past I suffered from acne. I remember being at a spa and my mother is there. She says: "You're so beautiful, your skin is so smooth!" Actually, I don't feel at ease, the way she looks at me makes me feel bad.

Interpretation: Nella's mother is like a baby, she never took care of her children. Nella has chosen to be a mother to take care of herself, as she felt she had been a motherless child. However, she is afraid of finding herself in the same situation as her mother and of rejecting her children. Her femininity is affected by an illness, a "cancer" to be kept under control with a pill. Nella is afraid of hurting her children and abandoning them just as her mother abandoned her.

> Third dream: You [therapist] and I lived together in the same bedroom with two small beds. I was twenty years old and we were in a village with my two eldest sons. You tell me to go and pick up the kids at school. While walking, I get lost, and you say "I'll show you the way." You open a green and white door for me and there are stairs going down. You say: "Don't be afraid." At the end of the stairs there is another door. We go out into the centre of town and there is a rail, behind it a gully. You let yourself down and you get to the school. There are ropes, I am afraid, I don't want to let myself down. I am "reticent"; no, I actually meant resistant! My children arrive and I ask: "How did you convince them to climb up?" "If they have learned to come to you, you needn't go to them", the therapist says in the dream.

Interpretation: the dream is evidently about therapy. An alliance has somehow been established with the therapist, and from that moment on she always appears in dreams. The relationship with her therapist is supposed to help Nella to find her children and take care of them. At the same time, though, what emerges is a strong wish for somebody else to take care of them and Nella's resistance to go towards them. In the dream she puts several barriers between her and her children, and sometimes it seems impossible to cover the distance between them. It is as if Nella wanted to be twenty again, in her young woman's bedroom. Accordingly, also in her therapy she wants to find a space of her own as a child and not only as a mother. She cannot admit that she would leave her children on the other side of the gully! She is ambivalent towards them.

> Fourth dream: I was huddled in a corner, in lilac pajamas and you were next to me and you said: "You do have emotions, you just have to allow yourself to feel them!" I felt pervaded by beautiful emotions, full of colours, and I said: "What I have been missing till now!" And I thought: "Maybe I could feel like this for someone."

Interpretation: Nella is feeling better, she takes care of herself and, since she has more time for herself and a space of her own, she has overcome her ambivalence towards her children. When she is at home, she is calmer and more helpful than before, but she accepts that she can also leave.

Betti

> First dream: A sensation of strong impotence. I want to open my mouth, but it won't open. The upper part and the mandible stick onto the lower teeth. I feel the lower canine tooth is dangling and it comes off, like a milk-tooth. The canine has a hole in it, it is empty because it has been smashed by the upper teeth. I keep on smashing my molar teeth, and they flake off. "Oh God, what am I doing?" I am frightened, but the mandible seems automatic, out of control. It is as if the ceiling were tumbling down on me.

Betti's comments and suggestions deriving from the dream: "What is strange is that when I woke up, my muscles didn't ache. Since that day, though, my neck and mandible have been aching." The symptoms of mandibular pain and contracture with teeth grinding in sleep begins at the age of fifteen, and now Betty is twenty-seven. She says that her mandible is her capacity to control, to be silent and avoid others. Being silent and keeping her secrets, lying and not talking about her personal life, is very important for her, as it means avoiding the judgment of others—which she strongly fears. "I have always felt judged by my father, to him I was always wrong. If I don't say anything, people won't judge me." She also adds that she fears others' being aggressive, and that she can only go away to defend herself. In her vision, the empty canine, similar to a milk-tooth, stands for her difficulty in using her teeth, that is, being aggressive—which can sometimes help, especially at work.

CHAPTER TWELVE

Healing and the end of therapy

The concept of healing and mental health

Psychotherapy is supposed to end when the objectives established in the contract are achieved, and, consequently, when the problems due to which one began one's personal analysis and one's treatment path are solved. The therapist and the patient both have in mind an idea of how therapy is supposed to end and it is important to explore these representations and make them explicit.

For the therapist, the idea of the end of the therapy is associated with the theoretical model she is following, as this model generally includes in its guidelines ideal levels of maturity, healing, and autonomy. Besides, the therapist is also conditioned by her personal ideals and philosophical inspirations, and by the concept of health and change that she pursues.

For the patient and client, the idea of the end of therapy is more subjectively connoted and must be explored from the very beginning, during the phase in which the therapeutic contract is defined.

During therapy, as well as in scientific debates and symposiums, there may be difficulty and reticence in speaking about healing; however, in Transactional Analysis we should find it easier to place the therapist–patient relationship in the Adult–Adult mode and to acknowledge that if this takes place we are already at a resolutive phase of the therapy, when the "mourning" for the perfect Parent–Child relationship has passed, and when the patient can accept his internal reality (his own self) and the external one (his relationships) for what they are.

For most people, healing means growing up, giving up their childish illusions and demands and managing to get by in the "grown-up" world by their own efforts and thanks to the support of other, a support exchanged on the basis of a principle of mutuality.

Mutuality means relationships in which giving and taking are balanced and imply free choice and the possibility of also making gifts.

Healing thus means accepting the human condition of being-in-the-world, of existing, of being thrown into the world, of being able to make projects within boundaries that are not completely determined by us, like our birth and our death, as described by Heidegger (1962).

Berne wrote that "the therapist should remember that while death is a tragedy, life is a comedy (furthermore, even one's own death is not always a tragedy as such; it may only become tragic in its effects on others). Curiously enough, many patients reverse this dramatic principle and treat life as a tragedy and death as a comedy. The therapist who follows them is once more a party to a folie à deux" (Berne, 1966, p. 289).

Keith Tudor, TA training analyst, would say that healing also means discovering the condition of we-ness, our being ourselves that constitutes our being men and women beyond the dual condition of you and I (Tudor & Summers, 2005).

Healing thus means basically learning a functional adaptation to life.

Adapting means conforming. Is this the recipe for our mental health?

We can say, though, that a person cannot be healthy within an unhealthy and unbalanced social system.

Sometimes, individual madness is the healthiest form of rebellion against the collective madness of history and of systems.

Madness can also be seen as a form of rebellion against and maladjustment to a negative adult life, an individual refusal to adapt on behalf of the adolescent, a sometimes desperate form of retreat and rebellion.

This theme of rebellion and refusal is often explicitly present in adolescents' mental illnesses, in drug addiction, in eating disorders, and in depressions.

On the one hand, it is difficult to leave the safe world of childhood to join the unstable and uncertain world of adults. On the other hand, adolescents rebel against their parents' lives, which look so mediocre and sad, and refuse to adapt to them. Unfortunately, sometimes the outcry is replaced by a silent moan of those who say "I can't cope", which is much sadder.

Assuming that social systems can be healthy or disturbed, a person's health and madness must accordingly be understood as complex interactions. If a social system is healthy, it respects human nature and individual subjectivities, accepts differences and allows communications and exchanges without expecting standardisations. It therefore also accepts illness and madness as human expressions, as expressions of the pursuit of a real life and of the striving it implies.

A society of the healthy and beautiful was the utopian ideal of the collective paranoia that nearly caused twentieth-century civilisation to collapse. It characterised the madness driving Hitler's Nazi regime and totalitarianism in all its expressions.

It is really very important for psychotherapy not to validate these delirious false myths.

There is not only one way to be mentally healthy, mature, or "healed".

Gabbard (2004) states that, during the therapy, the therapist who follows a dynamic approach searches in every patient for a unique subjective truth. She tries to recognise and validate the patient's real self.

This search for the real self represents, then, the objective of the analytic process, and healing thus consists in enabling the person to communicate with his real self, preferably without having to leave out the rest of the world or intimate relationships. Berne (1972) would say that therapy aims at turning the frog into a prince, as has previously been said. In order to do so, therapy must turn the patient inside out, help him to break out of his script and live in the real world. The antithesis of the script is the powerful message that the therapist gives as soon as the patient is ready to redecide, to be "turned inside out", to turn from patient to "real person impatient to leave".

All of this can happen in just one dialectic exchange, according to Berne, and, I add, if the patient is by then ready to accept both the message itself and how intensely this message can penetrate deep inside and be then kept inside as a permission and a blessing.

The end of therapy

How we meet people and say hello to them reveals a lot about our individual personality.

Following Berne's theories, we can say that how we say "goodbye" or "see you"—in other words how we separate from others—may reveal fundamental aspects of our life-scripts.

The way we get in touch with others, the way we create bonds and maintain them, and the way we say hello or goodbye are the three situations which reveal the essence of our interpersonal skills and, therefore, of our existing.

Similarly, in the therapeutic relationship, the moment of the end of therapy and of goodbyes is a fundamental phase of the process. It is very useful, then, to include this stage in the treatment path and analyse very carefully what happens over the last period of treatment.

Saying goodbye in the therapist–patient relationship is an experience to try, analyse, elaborate, we might say mentalise.

The therapist must announce that this moment is going to come, help the patient imagine it and anticipate it in his mind, to discuss it together and explore the different—and often ambivalent—feelings and thoughts that this moment arouses. It is a phase of analysis of the process of elaboration of the transference. In TA we would say it is like separating from a parent and leaving our mother's and father's house.

Everyone says goodbye in their own way

Actually, some people do not say goodbye at all and simply disappear, in order to avoid emotions related to separating. Some people fight, some disappear, some feel worse and consider it easier to leave, judging therapy ineffective.

Delia's case

Delia had been attending group therapy for three years. She confessed that she often dreamed about causing a row to interrupt the group and then going to an unknown therapist to tell her she was finally healthy. She said she felt a lonely pleasure when she imagined that she would not please her therapist. Overtly telling this fantasy was very helpful in Delia's therapy. She suffered from a borderline personality disorder and had serious conflicts with her mother, who had left her to her aunt from the age of three to six, while her two brothers had stayed within the family.

Hatred for her mother, envy towards her brothers, the illusion of her mother's eventually accepting and saving her in an illusory relationship—a relationship that Delia was not able to establish with anyone—accompanied her, and Delia often felt a terrible, destructive anger. Accordingly, her relationships were to contain the punishment she meant for her mother.

"It's your fault if I suffer so much, but as long as I suffer so much, you will have to take care of me. If I am ever to be fine, you will leave me, so I will never tell you I'm fine and I can get by on my own. You-mother and you-therapist will have to worry about me all your life, with your guilt at hurting me." When Delia was a six-year-old child, she had regained her place in her family, making terrible scenes at every party or meals with the whole family ("I ruined several Christmas parties") until her father finally took her back home. This conflictual and ambivalent model had been deeply projected on to the therapist and the group. In fact, Delia talked about her protests and complaints but not about her progress. After she had reported her fantasy about the end of therapy to the other members of the group, it was possible to elaborate the central aspects of her affective life-script.

Those patients who have negative transferences characterised by deep hatred, as Gabbard writes, try heavy second—and sometimes third—degree games at the end of the therapy. It is important to foresee the games likeliest to emerge in order not to be hooked, and also invite the patient to foresee, imagine, analyse, and elaborate these critical moments.

A bipolar patient could actually interrupt the pharmacological therapy responsible for his balance, thus bringing about a maniacal disturbance (I'm almighty, I no longer need anybody else) in order to disguise and not to confront the sadness due to separating.

The end of therapy certificate

Ending psychotherapy implies not only relational meanings. The end of therapy for many patients is like graduating from high school or university. It means concluding successfully a formative experience and attaining autonomy.

Most of all, it means that the attainment of autonomy is socially acknowledged: you are an adult and you are OK, you can take your decisions, you can make it, your guide is inside you and you no longer need an external guide. Of course, this achievement implies responsibilities that come with it, but it also allows a person to experience the pleasure of his own personal power.

The therapist who works according to this perspective must from the very beginning "stroke" the patient, who agrees to take on his responsibilities.

According to Berne, the ideal conclusion of script therapy is the condition of Integrated Adult. Similarly to what happens for the crew of a boat race, in order for the team to be well-balanced, the Adult I is firmly controlling the helm, while the Parent and Child dimensions are directed by the helmsman.

Berne described the functions of autonomy, spontaneity, and awareness as antithetic to being in a script, as these functions characterise the Integrated Adult.

Tudor (Tudor & Summers, 2005) speaks about the *Integrating* Adult, thus defining the ideal in terms of a dynamic, ever-changing process. The Adult as ego state will still integrate the introjected and archaic parts of the personality as they emerge.

This is the condition of an adult person who is psychically healthy, no longer coerced by his script, by a model based on archaic attachment that still affects present life.

The role of dreams in elaborating the end of therapy

Luisa is a young woman in her thirties. She is undergoing TA psychotherapy in an individual setting. Her personal story is one of adolescent depression associated with difficulties in spontaneous feeling and in expressing her thoughts assertively in academic contexts or in the workplace. In particular, she revised her relationship with her mother, as Luisa does not think she received support and confidence (my mother is a child).

Luisa's dream

> I'm standing in line at the airport to leave for Frankfurt on a school trip.

During the flight I see wonderful things: a context of coloured sand-castles.

We stop over in Paris and it's late. It's 3.45 p.m. and my odyssey begins.

You [therapist] are there, and you say that it's not late!

I'm breathless, and I'm carrying several backpacks full of bits and bobs.

I haven't got my boarding card, it's the wrong one.

So they tell me: Give us your identity card.

But I have my brother's.

You were there and said: I'll see you on Wednesday. You reassure me.

So I leave, and everybody is friendly to me. I was the only one to be upset.

I hugged you before I left.

Analysis of Luisa's dream:

I know I'm supposed to take off, and I see you as someone to count on. You accompany me.

Paris was my first trip abroad, on a school trip.

Frankfurt, for me, symbolises independence and autonomy.

Wednesday is the day I was born, and it's a good omen.

Luisa is about to end her therapy! Her dream shows the mentalisation of this phase of the process. Luisa is afraid of departures and separations from others because she remembers that her adolescence was a chaotic and confused period (her backpack full of bits and bobs) and a period in which she felt lost, without identity (I have the wrong boarding card, it's my brother's).

The meeting with the therapist in her dream enables her to rely on herself, to retrieve the day she was born (her real self) and so the possibility to leave for Frankfurt (symbol of autonomy, Adult journey)

Magic expectations, healing from transferences and delusion

Berne (1966, p. 284) wrote that "the main problem of psychotherapy is that at a deeper level the patient comes to the therapist hoping that if he/she behaves in a certain way and follows the therapist's instructions, the therapist will eventually give the patient the magic orb, and in that way he/she will obtain its permanent possession". Berne adds that one of the distressful tasks of the therapist is telling the patients that Santa Claus does not exist.

I remember a patient who came back to me for a follow-up several years after the end of the therapy and told me that she had stopped believing in God and "behaving well" because she had not been rewarded for the commitment and honesty that had always characterised her life. Someone in her family had fallen ill with cancer, and she had not won an important competition for a job, so she felt that she was being punished and that it was not fair. She imagined that life was ruled by an external judge who assigned prizes and punishments according to supreme justice. Her attending psychotherapy also caused disappointment, as if supreme justice did not recognise and reward the commitment with which she faced every trial.

Even though explicit accusations against therapy had not been made, I could feel a slight resentment towards it during the dialogue.

I felt that this patient was conveying anger, resentment, as if she were saying: what you taught me is not enough to make me succeed and protect me from pain.

Some patients decide to interrupt therapy when they find out that they are not going to get the orb, and they may end the therapy in anger and with accusations against the therapist.

Other patients end therapy at a hypomanic phase; they feel they are Santa Claus themselves. Others are willing to revise these fantasies and expectations in therapy.

Thinking of a hypothetical patient, Berne added that:

> the reason he can be "cured" is that while one part of him clings to the Santa Claus fantasy and would rather live in a fairy-tale world than give up hope, some other part of him knows it is an illusion. [...] the therapist can offer him the whole real world to replace the lost illusion, new lamps for old nostalgias, a fresh red apple for a vanished orb.
>
> Transactionally, what actually happens in this framework is as follows: the patient comes to the therapist with the idea that the therapist has the patient's cure at his disposal, probably locked in his desk. It is only because the therapist is demanding, stingy, mean or selfish, that he doesn't hand it to the patient immediately

at the first interview, but the patient has little doubt at first that if he behaves well enough for long enough, it will be given to him, very much as Santa Claus would give him presents when he was little. (Berne, 1966, pp. 284–285)

At the final phase of therapy, the therapist must encourage the patient to explore these issues, even if they do not spontaneously emerge. This is mainly because fantasies and experiences related to how patients end therapy, and the way the patient thinks of himself after the therapy, are a good feedback of the change that has been undertaken.

If one has an integrated and integrating Adult, the mourning process for the loss of Santa Claus will have been completed and the patient will be able to use humour—which Berne identifies as one of the healthy characteristics—with his therapist. In fact, in the final sessions we can use irony and teach the patient to smile at his illusions, which would have been completely inappropriate at the beginning phase with a suffering and contaminated patient. If we are at the end of therapy, in fact, "we laugh with him" and not "at him", as in the famous sentence of the teacher played by Robin Williams in the film *The Dead Poets' Society*.

> The biological or survival value of humor is to deal summarily with predicaments, thus releasing the individual to go about the business of living as effectively as he can under the circumstances. Since most psychogenic problems seem to arise from self-deception, Adult humour has a most rightful place in the *materia medica* of the psychotherapist. (Berne, 1966, p. 289)

In his wonderful book *The Developing Mind*, D. J. Siegel describes the forms of co-operative communication that generate secure attachment and he talks about the process of integration of the mind as one that is also allowed to grow and regenerate through psychotherapeutic treatment.

If therapy works, Siegel writes,

> This new capacity for integration—both interpersonal and internal—may create a sense of vitality and a release of creative energy and ideas, leading to an invigorating sense of personal expression. Such spontaneous and energized processes can give rise to participation in various activities, such as painting, music, dance,

poetry, creative writing or sculpture. It can also yield a deeper sense of creativity and appreciation within the "everyday" experience of life: communication with others, walks down the street, new appreciation of the richness of perceptions, feeling of being connected to the flow of the moment. (Siegel, 1999, p. 375)

And he adds:

It is in these heightened moments of engagements, these dyadic states of resonance, that one can appreciate the power of relationships to nurture and to heal the mind. (Siegel, 1999, p. 377)

CHAPTER THIRTEEN

Transactional Analysis: towards an ecology of social relationships*

A s counsellors, we meet people every day and take care of problems in workplaces, family relationships, and educational environments. This requires from us a continuous and keen analysis of our time, and of the most significant expressions of human joy and suffering, of fear and anger. We may say that our listening, analysing, and accompanying people makes us anthropologists and explorers involved in every human adventure.

Psychologists, educators, and counsellors often act as people who know where to go and what path is to be followed in order to appear healthy, happy, and free to the person who is in search of help, education, or guidance.

In truth, we are aware that we are neither gurus nor illuminated people and that we can support others only if we follow that guiding light which shows us the way even in these complex and disorienting times.

Our guiding light is, in effect, thought—albeit an intersubjective thought, due to the bond with the human communities to which we

---

*Pisa, Second PerFormat Conference, 17 October 2009.

belong. There, we learn to express ourselves spontaneously, thanks to our relationships with others, which, like a mirror, show us the process of truly becoming men and women in the world.

With Hannah Arendt, we say that plurality constitutes the real substance of being man or woman.

Living in a hurry

Our world has been defined by sociologists as "the world of liquid modernity". This metaphor of sea and water invites us to consider instability not as a limit but merely as the different consistency of our surrounding environment.

Bauman (2000), one of the greatest contemporary sociologists, coined this phrase. He uses the concept of liquidity to describe the velocity and rapidity that characterise the processes of social change.

In the time of liquid modernity, in our postmodern era, being in a hurry and being ahead of others is what consumer society demands (the "cutting edge look" that will make other people look up to you: it is the most convincing of advertisements).

Being ahead and staying ahead is the only way to be respected, and to be one of those who count. We need to keep constantly up to date with new trends and novelties, because novelties quickly wear off, and one can, and must, choose—only among the ready-made looks we are offered, though.

Modern man's condition is thus characterised by a perpetual state of emergency, constant movement, and rapid learning.

However, "consuming life cannot be other than a life of rapid learning, but it also needs to be a life of swift forgetting", Bauman (2007, p. 96) writes.

Thus, the paradox of consumer society is that, although it seems to be based on the attempt to satisfy one's needs, it actually thrives as long as it manages to render the non-satisfaction of its members: only someone who is not satisfied is continuously in search of new trends and new seasons.

A person who is satisfied is an imperfect consumer and must therefore become a social outcast.

The appeal of ever-fleeting happiness is a good omen in a consumer economy, as it calls for another round of shopping. In this society, not only do we need to produce and purchase, but also to discard and start over again.

Think of how successful *feng-shui* and space clearing—which teaches us how to get rid of all the things we have filled our houses with over the years—have been, and how much money people spend in order to clear their minds from the burden of too many emotions and thoughts with the help of psychologists or oriental disciplines.

Companies specialising in selling durable goods have learned this lesson too: they charge their customers, not for delivery, but for disposal of those goods to be replaced, such as an old electrical appliance or a car to be scrapped.

Companies selling personal services also specialise in excision: body fat, hairs, acne, depression, and so on.

Even relationships must be something one can easily get rid of: in a survey from Bath University, one third of the students interviewed stated that they do not mind breaking up a relationship just by sending a text message.

Eriksen writes that even the here and now is nowadays threatened by the next moment, which comes so quickly that it becomes difficult to live the present: "The consequences of this extreme hurriedness are overwhelming: both the past and the future as mental categories are threatened by the tyranny of the moment" (Eriksen, 2001, p. 3).

According to Bauman, our society needs people who live without paying attention to past experiences or future consequences of current actions, and that such frailty is represented as the substance of individual freedom.

Ramonet writes that more information has been produced in the last thirty years than during the previous 5000 and that "a single copy of the New York Times contains more information than a cultivated person in the XVIII century would consume during a lifetime" (Ramonet, 1999, p. 184).

According to Eriksen, in order to live healthily we should get rid of 99.99% of all the information we are offered!

What about us?

We have to help people find their way in this ocean of information, and enable them to construct a narrative in which past, present, and future are continuous and meaningful, in which the presence of others creates a bond, and does not represent mere company or an empty reflection of themselves which only gives rise to competition.

We listen to many people, to their experiences of unrest and uneasiness. We know that identities are nowadays often fragmented, that the most common pathologies are borderline or narcissistic personalities, and that manifestations of anxiety or panic are associated with dependence disorders.

Dealing with people's sufferance, confused minds, and interrupted dialogues, we can deeply understand our times.

In every historical period, psychic disorders have mirrored the unease of that particular time and the difficulties of common people, as well as the protest of those who just cannot go with the times or simply refuse to do so.

What does "to cure" mean, then? In our conception, it cannot be translated into silencing this individual protest, nor into letting people surrender to conformism or to the levelling condition of being all alike.

For us, to cure means, first of all, to listen to screams, silence, and sobs with deep respect and to accept a confused search for meaning whose purpose is to confer dignity to "him who strives", as Goethe wrote in his *Faust*.

"He who strives on and lives to strive/Can earn redemption still", the angels declare as they eventually take Faust up to Heaven.

People who strive to understand their lives, to confer meaning on their suffering, and are willing to do so within the relational space of counselling and psychotherapy, are not in search of a happiness pill, they are ready to face a path of introspection and growth in which they are prepared to take responsibility for deep thoughts and confrontation.

Counselling and psychotherapy, in our view, are paths of training and learning, paths of empowerment. Being empowered means being able to make choices and act consistently and properly.

Bauman writes:

> Authentic empowerment means that people not only acquire the abilities necessary to successfully play in a game projected by others, but also the power necessary to influence the objectives, the stakes and the rules of the game: not only personal ability but social power. Empowerment requires the building and rebuilding of inter-human bonds, the will and the ability to engage with others in

a continuous effort to make human cohabitation into a hospitable and friendly setting for the mutually enriching cooperation of men and women struggling for self-esteem, for the development of their potential and for the proper use of their abilities. (Bauman, 2005, p. 98)

A pause in our pursuit of happiness

Does one go to a counsellor or a psychologist to find happiness?

Bauman suggests calling for a pause in this frenetic and spasmodic chase: a pause means acquiring a healthy, critical point of view of this pursuit of standardised happiness.

In TA we say that a winning script is not represented by economic and social success, but by the achievement of personal objectives; after all, it consists of a constructive life according to one's own subjectivity. Not always can the value of something be measured according to traditional criteria.

We can read in Robert Kennedy's speech delivered shortly before his assassination in 1968:

The gross national product does not allow for the health of our children, the quality of their education or the joy of their play. It does not include the beauty of our poetry or the strength of our marriages, the intelligence of our public debate or the integrity of our public officials. It measures neither our wit nor our courage, neither our wisdom nor our learning, neither our compassion nor our devotion to our country, it measures everything in short, except that which makes life worthwhile.

What kind of happiness do we help people to pursue and to achieve, then? We encourage people to follow training paths and research paths where they can learn to live with their own inner worlds of thoughts and emotions, discover how to listen to the sounds of life and to the voices of others, and enjoy life in its development, with that same curiosity and capacity to be surprised and moved by it as a child.

Is it possible to plan our lives nowadays?

Years ago, lab mice in the labyrinth learned adaptation strategies, and adapted so as to survive: the condition of human life was similar. In our time, in order for this comparison to be true, the labyrinth should be virtual, the sections should be on wheels so as to be moved at every new attempt, and the prizes should be left in different places every time.

Long-term adaptation is not possible nowadays. In a world like ours, making long-term projects can be risky. Each identity is fleeting, vulnerable, and fragile, and the compulsion of our consumer society is subtle but deeply and inwardly manipulative.

No one is forced to frenetically chase the latest trends, but nonetheless people do, in order to feel that they belong and they are OK.

Projects are thus fragmentary and objectives are forever changing their position.

From roots to anchors

Nowadays, the most effective metaphor to describe the human need for bonds and belonging is no longer the metaphor of roots—which implies the trauma of being uprooted—but that of anchors that will be cast and weighed over and over, in de Singly's words (2003). As a matter of fact, weighing an anchor does not represent a definitive choice.

In the life of every person there is an inevitable creative aspect and co-creative need based on prior commitment towards others.

Do we really have to pursue renewal and innovation? If so, why?

As for individuals, then, is it important to renew oneself, to rebuild continuously, and to reconstruct oneself?

There is positive and negative stability in personal identity: the sense of continuity represents the positive part, while what is defective is the rigidity stemming from fixed beliefs and experiences connected with the past.

There is negative instability in modern liquidity—and that is the process of crumbling and the tyranny of the moment—but also positive instability, represented by the capacity to constantly grow and learn.

We cannot, therefore, speak of compulsion to innovation and renewal, but of flexibility as possibility and openness to novelties—and this is creation and co-creation.

Utopias and fears are no longer those told by Huxley and Orwell, but those expressed by Michel Houellebecq (2005) in *The Possibility of an Island*, set in the future, in a place inhabited by a new race of beings, clones of ancient original humans who achieved immortality thanks to technological asexual reproduction of themselves. In this scenario, Daniel 24 and Daniel 25, clones of the ancient Daniel 1, find the diaries of their ancestor who lived in our time, and in those pages they read a pitiless and desolate account of the decadency and end of a world, our world.

Choosing

If you think it is possible to make the world anew and turn it into a different world, a more peaceful, friendlier, and warmer place for human beings ... then you do believe that you have a chance to make a difference: a difference for your life, but also for the world you live in. Life, human life, can be but a work of art. Will and choice do leave their mark on a form of life.

Life is lived in uncertainty. There is not a simple and unambiguous way to avoid choosing and starting a path. Identity is not given—it is, on the contrary, created like a work of art.

"Our lives, whether we know it or not and whether we relish the news or bewail it, are works of art. To live our lives as the art of life demands, we must, just like the artists of any art, set ourselves challenges which are difficult to confront point-blank; we must choose targets that are well beyond our reach, and standards of excellence that vexingly seem to stay stubbornly far above our ability to match whatever we do or may be doing", Bauman states (2008, pp. 19–20).

There *are* some points of reference that, just like a compass, help modern sailors to find their way through this liquid world. Seamen always have reference points; those who get lost on a sea journey are those who do not rely either on the position of stars or sun, or on a compass—or GPS, we might say nowadays.

There is thus a network that helps a person be aware of his position on his journey, and for us this basically consists in our being there for others.

An ethic for sailors

There is an ethic which is central to our time, as it accepts uncertainty but nonetheless enables us to find our way.

Emmanuel Lévinas is one of the great masters who can guide us along this path: he is the one who founded the ethics of responsibility.

Responsibility for the Other is the main, fundamental, essential structure of subjectivity.

I am inasmuch as I am for the Other.

As soon as the Other's face penetrates my eyes, I am offered the possibility to escape the isolation of *existing* and enabled to *be*. Responsibility, as described by Lévinas, precedes intentional consciousness. It is inevitable, it is the intersubjectivity we are moulded in and made of as human beings: "Intersubjective relationship is a non-symmetrical relationship. In this sense, I am responsible for the Other without waiting for reciprocity, even if I were to die for it" (Lévinas, 1969, pp. 193–194).

When this dimension is lost, our being human itself is lost, and we become mere objects. Many healthcare professionals who work in emergency departments have told me of their concern about the coldness and lack of empathy (described in Latin by the term *pietas*) that they have witnessed over the last years. Sometimes, somebody is dying and, instead of silence and respect, these are the words the assistants hear: "Does one have to die to attract your attention? Hurry up, I have to be back at work in an hour!"

The ancient and traditional *pietas* gives rise to primary empathy, spontaneous smiles, and the impulse to go towards the Other which we may now explain in terms of mirror neurons and theories on the intersubjective mind. It is this very impulse that we have to reactivate when it dies down, because reactivating it means coming back to life and perceiving it as an authentic work of art. It is the only salvation from isolation and cure for the tragedy and the coldness of pathological narcissism or the fragmented and crumbled identity typical of postmodern borderline cases.

It is for these reasons that training and therapy groups are necessary, as are people who inspire, guide, and accompany us along our path and the experience of words and values that make human life more colorful. This is increasingly true, more than in the past, since it is during a journey that one discovers what is essential and gets rid of the superfluous; and currently we are on a constant journey, constantly in need of finding the essential, and travelling with our hand baggage only, light, and therefore essential.

REFERENCES

Adler, A. (1936). On the interpretation of dreams. *International Journal of Individual Psychology, 2:* 3–16.

Arendt, H. (1957). *The Human Condition.* Chicago: The University of Chicago Press.

Bauman, Z. (2000). *Liquid Modernity.* Cambridge: Polity Press.

Bauman, Z. (2005). *Liquid Life.* Cambridge: Polity Press.

Bauman, Z. (2007). *Consuming Life.* Cambridge: Polity Press.

Bauman, Z. (2008). *The Art of Life.* Cambridge: Polity Press.

Berne, E. (1963). *The Structure and Dynamics of Organizations and Groups.* New York: Lippincott.

Berne, E. (1964). *Games People Play.* New York: Grove Press.

Berne, E. (1966). *Principles of Group Treatment.* New York: Grove Press.

Berne, E. (1968). *A Layman's Guide to Psychiatry and Psychoanalysis.* New York: Simon & Schuster.

Berne, E. (1972). *What Do You Say After You Say Hello? The Psychology of Human Destiny.* New York: Grove Press.

Calvino, I. (1988). *Six Memos for the Next Millennium.* Cambridge, MA: Harvard University Press.

Clarkson, P., & Fish, S. (1988). Rechilding. Creating a new past in the present as a support for the future. *Transactional Analysis Journal (TAJ), 18:* 51–59.

de Singly, F. (2003). *Les uns avec les autres*. Paris: A. Colin.

Eriksen, T. H. (2001). *Tyranny of the Moment: Fast and Slow Time in the Information Age*. London: Pluto Press.

Erskine, R. (1997). *Theories and Methods of an Integrative Transactional Analysis*. San Francisco: TA Press.

Fairbairn, W. R. D. (1952). *Psychoanalytic Studies of the Personality*. London: Tavistock.

Fosshage, J. L. (1983). The psychological function of dreams. A revised psychoanalytic perspective. *Psychoanalysis and Contemporary Thought, 6*: 641–669.

Freud, S. (1900a). *The Interpretation of Dreams. S. E., 4–5*. London: Hogarth.

Freud, S. (1916b). *Introductory Lectures on Psycho-analysis. S. E., 15*. London: Hogarth.

Fromm, E. (1951). *The Forgotten Language: An Introduction to the Understanding of Dreams, Fairy Tales and Myths*. New York: Grove Press.

Gabbard, G. O. (2000). *Psychodynamic Psychiatry in Clinical Practice*. Washington, DC: American Psychiatric Press.

Gabbard, G. O. (2004). *Long Term Psychodynamic Psychotherapy*. Arlington, VA: American Psychiatric Publishing.

Gibran, K. (1991). *The Prophet*. London: Pan.

Greenberg, R., & Perlman, C. (1993). An integrated approach to dream theory. In: A. Moffit, M. Kramer, & R. Hoffmann (Eds.), *The Function of Dreaming* (pp. 363–380). Albany, NY: State University of New York Press.

Hartmann, E. (1973). *The Function of Sleep*. New Haven, CT: Yale University Press.

Heidegger, M. (1962). *Being and Time*. New York: Harper & Row.

Houellebecq, M. (2005). The Possibility of an Island (trans. G. Bowd). London: Weidenfeld & Nicolson.

Jaspers, K. (1969). *Philosophy*. Chicago: The University of Chicago Press.

Jung, C. G. (1916). General Aspect of dream psychology. In: *The Structure and Dynamics of the Psyche. Collected Works. Vol. 8* (pp. 237–280). New York: Pantheon, 1960.

Kennedy, R. F. (1968). Remarks at the University of Kansas, 18 March. University of Kansas Library. Text available at http://www.jfklibrary.org/Research/Research-Aids/Ready-Reference/RFK-Speeches/

Kohut, H. (1977). *The Restoration of the Self*. New York: International Universities Press.

Lazarus, R. S. (1991). *Emotion and Adaptation*. London: Oxford University Press.

Lévinas, E. (1969). *Totality and Infinity: An Essay on Exteriority*. Pittsburgh: Duquesne University Press.

Maslow, A. H. (1962). *Toward a Psychology of Being*. New York: Van Nostrand.

Moiso, C., & Novellino, M. (2000). An overview of the psychodynamic school of transactional analysis and its epistemological foundations. *Transactional Analysis Journal (TAJ)*, 30: 182–187.

Novellino, M. (Ed.) (1998). *L'approccio clinico della Analisi Transazionale: epistemologia, metodologia e psicopatologia clinica*. Milan: Franco Angeli.

Novellino, M. (2004). *Psicoanalisi transazionale*. Milan: Franco Angeli.

Novellino, M. (2012). *The Transactional Analyst in Action: Clinical Seminars*. London: Karnac Books.

PDM Task Force (2006). *Psychodynamic Diagnostic Manual (PDM): A New Approach to Diagnosis in Psychotherapy*. Silver Spring, MD: Alliance of Psychoanalytic Organizations.

Propp, V. Y. (1958). *Morphology of the Folktale*. Bloomington, ID: Indiana University Research Center in Anthropology.

Ramonet, I. (1999). *La Tyrannie de la communication*. Paris: Galilée.

Siegel, D. J. (1999). *The Developing Mind*. New York: Guilford.

Steiner, C. (1974). *Scripts People Live: Transactional Analysis of Life Scripts*. New York: Grove Press.

Stern, D. (2004). *The Present Moment in Psychotherapy and Everyday Life*. New York: Norton.

Tuckman, B. W. (1977). Stages of small group development revisited. *Groups and Organizations Studies*, 2: 419–427.

Tudor, K., & Summers, G. (2005). Co-creative Transactional Analysis. In: B. Cornell & H. Hargaden (Eds.), *From Transactions to Relations: The Emergence of a Relational Tradition in Transactional Analysis*. Chipping Norton: Haddon Press.

INDEX